# BRITAIN BY NUMBERS

## A VISUAL EXPLORATION OF PEOPLE AND PLACE

# BRITAIN BY NUMBERS

## A VISUAL EXPLORATION OF PEOPLE AND PLACE

### STUART NEWMAN

Atlantic Books
London

# CONTENTS

# HOUSE AND HOME

# EDUCATION AND EMPLOYMENT

# PERSONAL FINANCE

# HEALTH AND FITNESS

# CRIME

# SOCIETY AND ECONOMICS

# LIFESTYLE AND LEISURE

# INTRODUCTION

'Lies, damn lies and statistics' is a popular refrain among those who ignore the numbers. Or maybe those who don't agree with the story they tell.

Either way, this book takes two differing views. Firstly, it sets out the statistics – the important data that shine a light on the UK, our fellow citizens, where we are and where we've been. Secondly, the descriptions provide context for the data's collection, what the data actually tell us and, sometimes, what level of trust we should place in these numbers.

The book is divided into chapters that reflect different aspects of our lives, covering subjects like leisure, family life, work, health and crime. I've sometimes used Britain as a substitute for the UK, although the former is a geographic term that excludes Northern Ireland while the latter is inclusive and political. In the course of writing this book I've learned a lot, not least that for the price of a flat in Chelsea you could buy roughly eight-and-a-half houses in Burnley, Lancashire; or that we spend nearly £500 million a year on treats for our dogs... From a logistical standpoint, I've realised how much of the data we see is focused on England and Wales. Scotland and Northern Ireland produce many of their own statistics and sometimes the three collection bodies have different aims, methodologies and data breakdowns, making it challenging to create UK-wide numbers, which I have done wherever possible. It has been an eye-opening journey and the result, I hope, is a fascinating and colourful tour up and down the land, which will improve our understanding of life in Britain.

Of the two different views outlined above, the statistics make up the bulk of this book. These data mostly come from 'official' sources – that is, government departments and agencies, especially the Office for National Statistics (ONS). There are various reasons for this, not least the fact that I work at the ONS so I'm more familiar with the statistical information, where its strengths lie and what it tells us. The second reason is that government has more access to our data than any other organisation. Think about it: the people who know the most about your salary are you, your company and the tax office, HMRC.

In fact, HMRC might actually understand your pay cheque better than you do. Furthermore, the government is the only UK organisation that can use the law to force companies to complete surveys. Even international bodies like the United Nations rely on national statistical institutions, such as the ONS, to provide their data.

That doesn't mean that the government is the best source of data for every topic. Industry bodies, consultancies, academics and other private organisations collect data that are useful for understanding elements of life in the UK. Some of those organisations are represented in these pages. But they collect data for different purposes – to promote an idea or element related to their work or to service their customer base. This is valid and important, but it also means that the data must be considered in context before assessing what it tells us.

As well as the organisations noted above, private companies collect large amounts of data about us and this is extremely valuable (just look at Facebook's share price – it can only stay elevated if they are able to effectively use our data to provide relevant ads). The issue with these data is that they're proprietary and companies have a disincentive to share. They might release some report or other on something they have gleaned from our digits (or at least digits that relate to us), but rarely will we see the underlying data. That makes it difficult to get the whole context and to determine exactly what it means.

This all relates to the third reason for this book's reliance on official data: access. Publishing data is a public service and democratic governments take that service seriously. They make data widely available and easy to reproduce.

But just because data come from an official source, it does not follow that we should accept it blindly. And this is the second element of this book. When the numbers say there's an increase in immigration, what should we read into that? On the face of it, more people are coming to the UK. But how are we measuring that? Are we missing anything? Are those figures reliable?

Getting answers to these queries sounds like a lot of work – sometimes we're bombarded by statistics. But getting into a habit of asking a few simple questions can lead to a much better understanding of the numbers: who collected the data, why and how?

So when a news report says that 'More than 7,000 people still watch TV in black and white', as the BBC did when I was writing this book, you can quickly discover that these data are collected by TV Licensing and are based on the number of black and white TV licences issued each year. Knowing that black and white TV licences are cheaper than their colourful cousins might lead you to ask whether some of those 7,000 people are cheating the system. All of this information was in the news story, just not the headline. My scepticism could be misplaced, but suddenly the numbers have other possible meanings.

Those same questions apply to all the data in this book and elsewhere in our lives. Throughout the book I've made reference to areas where we need to be cautious of how data are collected and whether the figures are robust. It's good to remember that data collected by surveys (which often rely on a sample of a population rather than a census) are usually estimates. That means they're inevitably wrong, but they may still be the best estimates we have. For data collected via another means (for example, public sector spending is based on the government's own accounts, which are widely available if a little difficult to understand) then the why and how questions above are key to determining reliability. The government knows how much it spends and it adheres to international accounting standards, interpretation of those standards notwithstanding. Furthermore, an independent government department with a regulator but no minister (i.e. the ONS, which is regulated by the UK Statistics Authority) interprets those accounting standards. So government finance numbers in this book are definitely robust. Although we're clearly unable to say that about all the data we see in the world.

So lies, damn lies and statistics? It's not quite as simple  as that – like the 7,000 or so black and white TVs in the UK, there are shades of grey. And possibly some other colours besides.

STUART NEWMAN

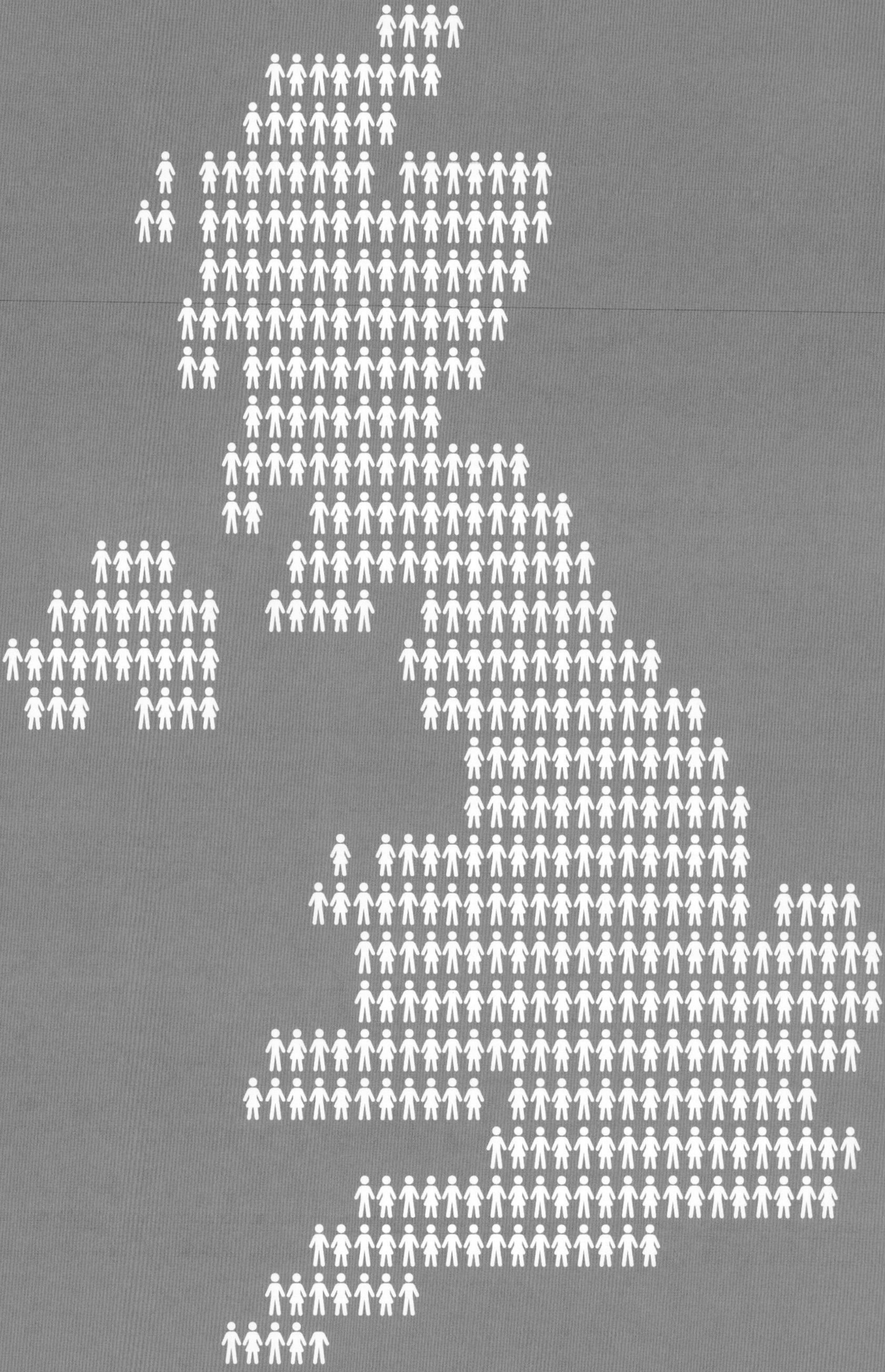

# 1

# WHO
# WE
# ARE

## POPULATION BY NUMBERS

There are various population themes throughout this book. We have an aging population with more people retiring than those entering work. And we're a nation of four countries, but England has more than five times as many people as the other three countries combined (and it's more densely populated). Yet there was one statistic that struck me more than most: every year there are more boys born than girls. UK (and presumably world) births average 51% male. Yet women are more populous in older cohorts. In 2017, the age at which gender numbers were most equal was 29. I have no idea why this is the case, but I like to think of it as nature's way of making up for adolescent testosterone overload.

\* See Notes for further details on this.
Data from 2017 rounded to the nearest thousand.

**29**

Age at which the number of women most closely matches the number of men (mid-year)

**3:1**

Ratio of employed people to retirees\*

**66,040**

TOTAL UK POPULATION

**102,000**

More boys than girls aged below five

**3,125,000**

Population of Wales

**223,000**

More women than men aged above 90

**5,425,000**

Population of Scotland

**,000**

# 1967

24% of people below 15
12% of people above 64

# 2017

18% of people below 15 (mid-year)
18% of people above 64 (mid-year)

**1,871,000**

Population of Northern Ireland

**55,619,000**

Population of England

# Halò

**57,000** people in Scotland speak some Gaelic

# Hullo

**1,538,000** people in Scotland speak some Scots

# Whit wey are ye

**35,000** people in N. Ireland speak some Ulster Scots

# Dia dhuit

**105,000** people in N. Ireland speak some Irish

# Helo

**1,119,000** people in Wales speak some Welsh

## FIRST LANGUAGES IN N. IRELAND

ENGLISH  1,681,000  97.5%

POLISH  18,000  1%

LITHUANIAN  6,000  0.4%

GAELIC (IRISH)  4,000  0.2%

PORTUGUESE  2,000  0.1%

SLOVAK  2,000  0.1%

## LANGUAGE IN BRITAIN

At school I had no interest in languages. I naively thought that everyone spoke English. This is not even true in the UK, let alone elsewhere in the world. Firstly, there are British languages, which have gone through a revival and are still spoken in pockets of the UK. Then there are languages that immigrants bring with them. And then there are the languages that we Brits learn.

We may be way behind some European neighbours with our language skills, but having learned basic Japanese I've come to realise that languages shape the way we think and they give you new insights into a culture. The lack of pronouns in Japanese, for example, puts less of a focus on the individual.

If we want to improve cultural understanding (which seems a noble aim), then improving foreign language skills is a good way to go.

Figures rounded to the nearest thousand. Main language data from 2011 census.

## FIRST LANGUAGES IN WALES

 ENGLISH OR WELSH*
2,871,000  93.7%

 POLISH  17,000  0.6%

 CHINESE  8,000  0.3%

 ARABIC  7,000  0.2%

 BENGALI  5,000  0.2%

TAGALOG  3,000  0.1%

\* Figures for English and Welsh are not split in the England and Wales Census data.

## FIRST LANGUAGES IN SCOTLAND

ENGLISH  4,741,000  92.6%

SCOTS  56,000  1.1%

POLISH  54,000  1.1%

CHINESE  31,000  0.6%

PUNJABI  26,000  0.5%

URDU  26,000  0.5%

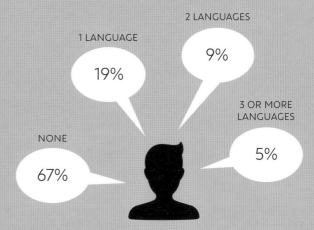

1 LANGUAGE
19%

2 LANGUAGES
9%

3 OR MORE LANGUAGES
5%

NONE
67%

HOW MANY SECOND
LANGUAGES DO YOU KNOW?
(answers from 2016)

## FIRST LANGUAGES IN ENGLAND

ENGLISH  46,937,000  88.4%

POLISH  529,000  1%

PUNJABI  272,000  0.5%

URDU  266,000  0.5%

BENGALI  216,000  0.4%

GUJARATI  212,000  0.4%

17

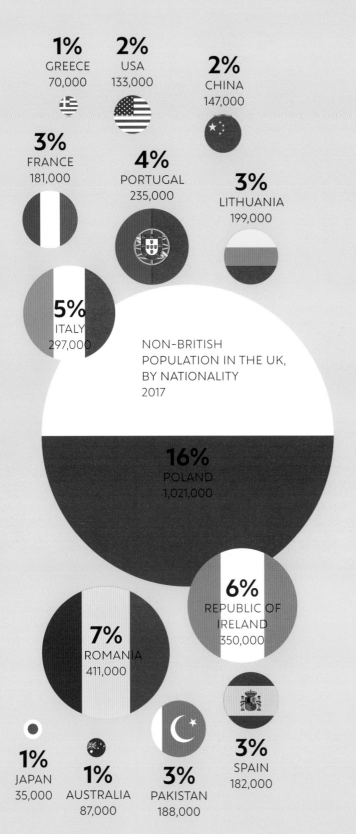

**1%**
GREECE
70,000

**2%**
USA
133,000

**2%**
CHINA
147,000

**3%**
FRANCE
181,000

**4%**
PORTUGAL
235,000

**3%**
LITHUANIA
199,000

**5%**
ITALY
297,000

NON-BRITISH
POPULATION IN THE UK,
BY NATIONALITY
2017

**16%**
POLAND
1,021,000

**6%**
REPUBLIC OF
IRELAND
350,000

**7%**
ROMANIA
411,000

**1%**
JAPAN
35,000

**1%**
AUSTRALIA
87,000

**3%**
PAKISTAN
188,000

**3%**
SPAIN
182,000

## IMMIGRATION

Immigrants have been coming to Britain for a long time and it has always been the case that immigrants have spread throughout the country. Yet London is a key focal point. More than a third of migrants who come to the UK settle in the capital and almost a quarter of London's population is non-British. Outside of London, the numbers tend to be relatively similar, with non-Brits making up a little less than 10% of the population.

These data represent a snapshot in time, and when looking at people's concerns around immigration they are usually around the flow of migrants in and out of the UK. But the level is important because there might be a connection between past migration and future migration. After all, it's easier to move to a new country if you already know people who live there. Yet this will be just one consideration for a potentially life-changing decision.

When migrants do come, it's interesting to see where they settle. Poles are the most common non-British resident in every region of the UK, but Romanians (the second most common non-British nationality living here) seem to have clustered more in certain English regions – London being an obvious example, but also the East and in the Midlands. Almost half of Italian immigrants live in London.

A little over half of all UK immigrants are women. Looking at the extremes, 3 out of every 4 Thai immigrants are women. So are 70% of Japanese immigrants and 60% of both Americans and Germans. At the other extreme, more than two-thirds of Iranian immigrants are men. And so are 3 out of 5 Albanians.

Data represent January to December 2017 (UK population is for mid-year 2017); rounded to the nearest thousand.

NON-BRITISH IN THE UK

**7%**
SCOTLAND
POPULATION
378,000

**7%**
NORTHERN
IRELAND
POPULATION
124,000

**90%**
OF NON-BRITISH
POPULATION
LIVE IN
ENGLAND

**4%**
WALES
POPULATION
135,000

**10%**
ENGLAND
POPULATION
5,573,000

**38%**
OF ENGLAND'S
IMMIGRANTS LIVE
IN LONDON
2,109,000

**6,210,000**
NON-BRITISH
POPULATION 2017
(UK POPULATION
66,040,000)

# UK AND NON-UK BORN

Every 10 years the Census gives us accurate population figures. For the years in between, we rely on survey samples to create estimated figures. When the next Census comes along, the Office for National Statistics will use the data to revise the survey-based estimates so that we get a more accurate figure for population numbers that make up each intervening year.

Using these methods, data on population are robust, especially when looking at large groups of

## 2004

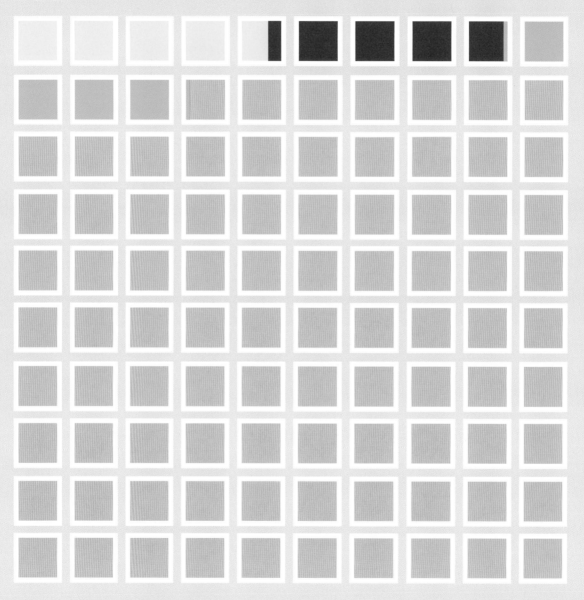

▦ White, UK born     ■ Non-white, UK born

people. Knowing that the data in these estimates are accurate, how multicultural is the UK?

We can say with confidence that 86% of the UK population was white in 2017. Also, 86% were UK born. Although these groups overlap, they're not a perfect match: 79% of people were white and UK born, with the other three groups (non-white UK born, and non-UK born, white and non-white) making up roughly 7% each. Is that more or less multicultural than you thought?

2017

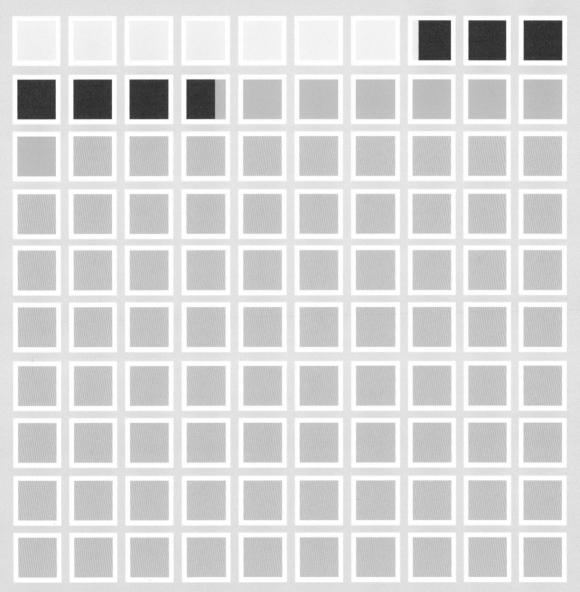

White, non-UK born          Non-white, non-UK born

# IMMIGRATION BY NUMBERS

Immigration has become a visceral topic in the UK. Yet often people form arguments that rely on aggregate figures only. There are nuances that are important for both sides of the debate. The data may be open to interpretation, but the first step is to look at the numbers. They might just change your opinion.

\* Figures rounded to the nearest 100.

## 3%

Total proportion of the world's migrants living in the UK (2017)

## 4.8%

Proportion of refugees in Europe that are in the UK (2017)

**EMIGRATION OUT OF ENGLAND (2016–2017)**

# 512, 302,

## 5,000

Net immigration into Wales (2016–2017)

## 15,000

Immigration into Wales (2016–2017)

## 10,000

Emigration out of Wales (2016–2017)

**33,000**
Immigration into Scotland
(2016–2017)

**20,000**
Emigration out of Scotland
(2016–2017)

**13,000**
Net immigration into Scotland
(2016–2017)

**000**
**000**

**IMMIGRATION
INTO ENGLAND
(2016–2017)**

**211,000**
Net immigration into England
(2016–2017)*

**11,000**
Immigration into Northern
Ireland (2016–2017)

**11,000**
Emigration out of Northern Ireland
(2016–2017)

**600**
Net immigration into Northern
Ireland (2016–2017)*

## MAJOR RELIGIONS

The UK is Christian, at least in theory. Christmas and Easter are national holidays; England and Scotland have their own Christian churches; 26 members of the House of Lords are Church of England Bishops; The Queen is Defender of the Faith and Supreme Governor of the Church of England and was blessed by the Church of Scotland post-coronation; 4 out of every 5 people in Northern Ireland follow a Christian religion; and close to 60% of people said they were Christian in the 2011 Census (after aggregating the results from the three Censuses: England and Wales, Scotland, and Northern Ireland).

Yet every major religion is represented in the UK. Close to 5 million people identified as belonging to a non-Christian religion in 2011. That said, almost 21 million failed to state any religion or said that they don't have a religion. I would guess that some of those with no religion celebrated Christmas last December – but it's also worth asking whether the 37 million who said they were Christian actually went to church last Sunday.

Data from 2011. Figures rounded to the nearest thousand.

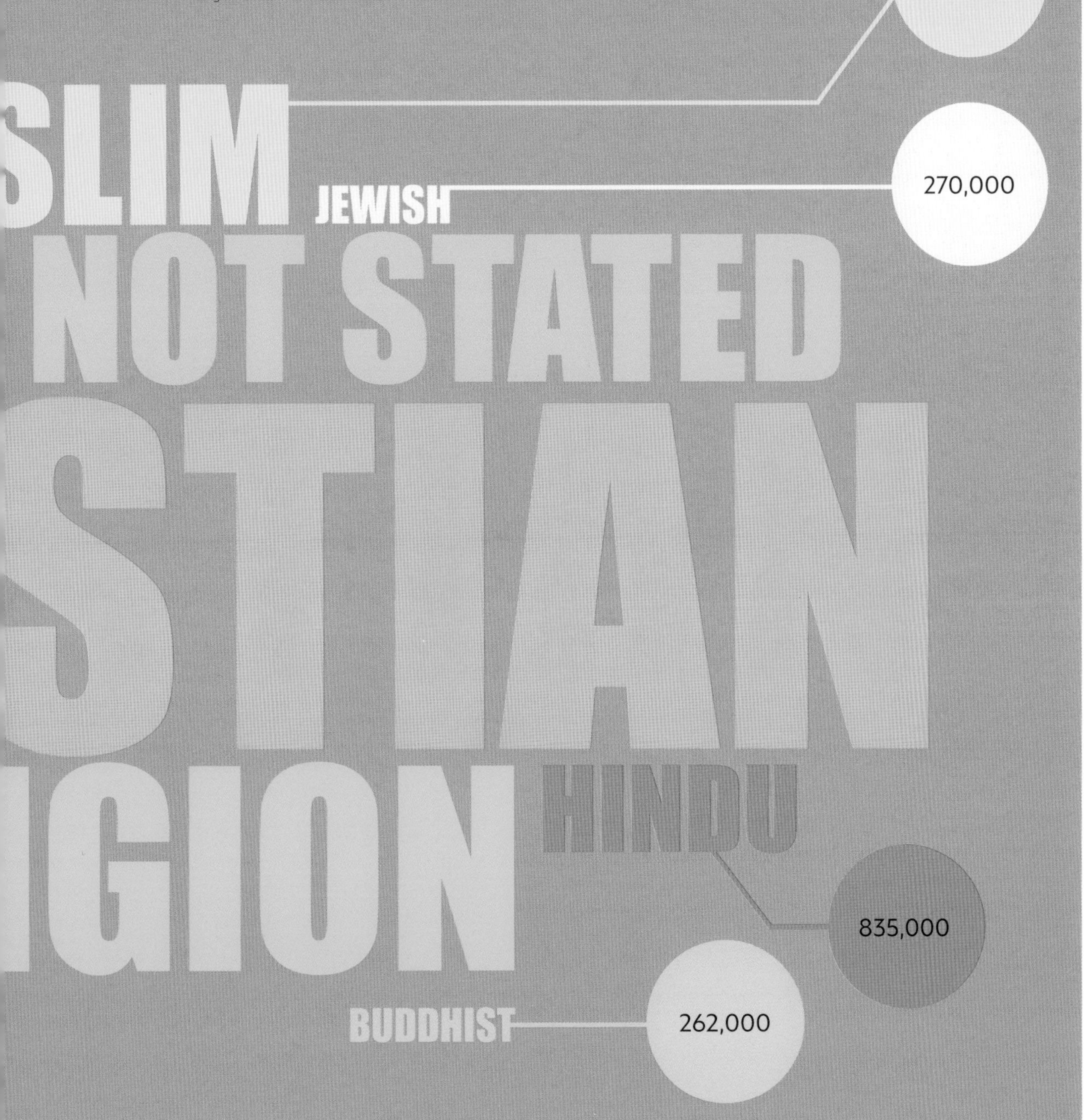

2,787,000

270,000

SLIM

JEWISH

NOT STATED

STIAN

IGION HINDU

835,000

BUDDHIST 262,000

# LOSING MY RELIGION

Christianity lost more than 10% of its followers in the decade between 2001 and 2011. That's two and a half times more than the gains in all the other religions combined. Some who decided not to give a religion (included in the 'no religion' category on this graphic) may well be Christians, but then there is a question over how many people are actually practising Christians. Maybe the 2011 figures represent an admission by millions of people that they were never really Christian in 2001 either. Presumably some Christians passed away in the interim and weren't replaced by younger entrants into the faith.

All other major religions succeeded in attracting new followers, though it's possible that immigration over the decade boosted their congregations.

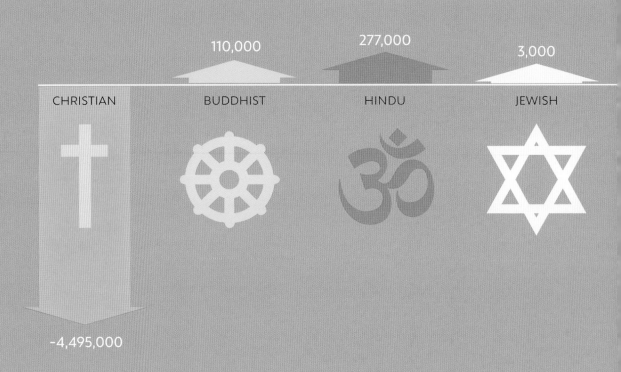

CHANGE IN RELIGIONS, 2001–2011

| CHRISTIAN | BUDDHIST | HINDU | JEWISH |
| --- | --- | --- | --- |
| | 110,000 | 277,000 | 3,000 |
| -4,495,000 | | | |

Buddhism and Islam both increased their numbers in the UK by more than 70%, Hinduism by 50% and Sikhism 30%. What's worrying for Christianity is that any immigration effect for other religions did not have the same effect for churches in the UK. This is surprising considering many Eastern European immigrants are likely to be Christian.

But a lot can happen in 10 years and it will be interesting to see how these figures have changed when the 2021 Census data become available.

Figures rounded to the nearest thousand.

7,124,000

1,196,000

96,000

84,000

MUSLIM                    SIKH                    OTHER                    NO RELIGION

# MINOR RELIGIONS

We're pretty proud of our sense of humour in Britain and in the 2011 Census we used the force to push 'Jedi Knight' up the list of religions. The Church (Temple? House?) of Jedi Knight is apparently more populous in the UK than that of Pagans (57,000), Humanists (15,000), Universalists and New Agers (each below 1,000).

I'm intrigued. I'd like to learn more, but I'm struggling to find a local congregation...

Excludes data for Scotland. Data from 2011.

2,462

SCIENTOLOGY

5,259

BAHA'I

30,278

ATHEIST

4,195

TAOIST

20,312

JAIN

6,301

HEAVY METAL

7,949

RASTAFARIAN

**1,924**

SATANISM

**178,094**

JEDI KNIGHT

**1,984**

HEATHEN

**4,120**

ZOROASTRIAN

# POPULATION DENSITY

The UK has a lot of beautiful countryside and spacious national parks, but few people live in these places and most of us are town and city dwellers. And these places can get crowded.

The crowds are more notable in England than in the other UK countries. In fact, every English region (for example, the South West, North East or Yorkshire and the Humber) is more densely populated than Northern Ireland, Wales or Scotland. And then there's London.

London is by far the most densely populated city in the UK. On a local authority (or equivalent) level, it has the 19 most densely populated areas in the UK. By the time you get to Liverpool on the list (number 35), you've already passed 26 of London's 33 boroughs. Now Liverpool is a large city and each London borough covers a much smaller area, so it's tempting to put the London-density dominance down to crowded areas being chopped up into more local authorities. That way they take up more space in the sample.

But Greater London is almost 30% more densely populated than Liverpool. The only city that comes close is Portsmouth with almost 5,400 people per square kilometre in 2016 compared with Greater London's 5,600. Those numbers might look similar, but 200 extra people living in a square kilometre is a lot – North Lincolnshire has about 200 people *in total* per square kilometre, for example.

For quieter parts of the UK it's best to head to Scotland, whose remote areas dominate the top 10 least populated local authorities. Eden in Cumbria and Powys in Wales are the only two non-Scottish locations to make the list. For Northern Ireland residents, Fermanagh and Omagh is the place to head for the quiet life (41 people per square kilometre).

Data from 2016 and by local authority or equivalent.

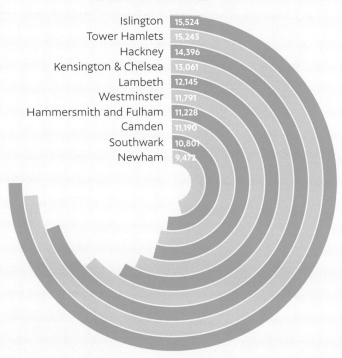

## MOST DENSELY POPULATED LOCAL AUTHORITIES

| | |
|---|---|
| Islington | 15,524 |
| Tower Hamlets | 15,243 |
| Hackney | 14,396 |
| Kensington & Chelsea | 13,061 |
| Lambeth | 12,145 |
| Westminster | 11,791 |
| Hammersmith and Fulham | 11,228 |
| Camden | 11,190 |
| Southwark | 10,801 |
| Newham | 9,473 |

## LEAST DENSELY POPULATED LOCAL AUTHORITIES

| | |
|---|---|
| Perth and Kinross | 29 |
| Powys | 26 |
| Eden | 25 |
| Scottish Borders | 24 |
| Dumfries & Galloway | 23 |
| Orkney Islands | 22 |
| Shetland Islands | 16 |
| Argyll & Bute | 13 |
| Na h-Eileanan Siar | 9 |
| Highland | 9 |

## POPULATION PER SQ KM

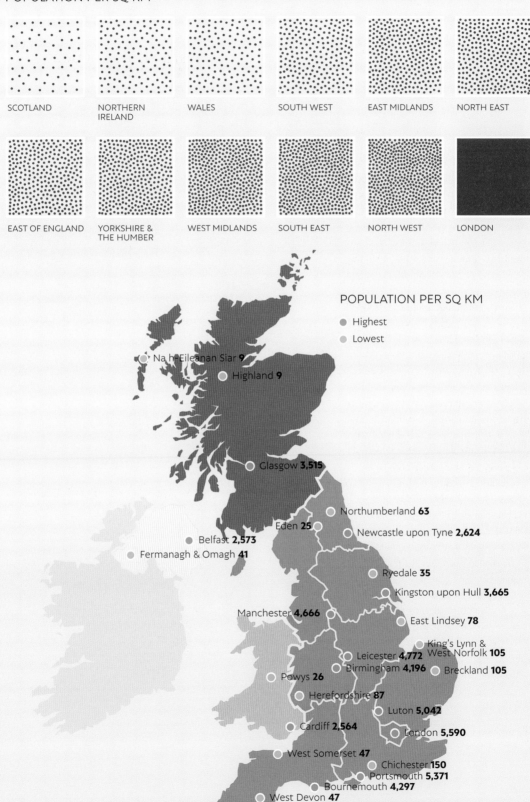

SCOTLAND

NORTHERN IRELAND

WALES

SOUTH WEST

EAST MIDLANDS

NORTH EAST

EAST OF ENGLAND

YORKSHIRE & THE HUMBER

WEST MIDLANDS

SOUTH EAST

NORTH WEST

LONDON

### POPULATION PER SQ KM

- Highest
- Lowest

Na h-Eileanan Siar **9**

Highland **9**

Glasgow **3,515**

Northumberland **63**

Eden **25**

Newcastle upon Tyne **2,624**

Belfast **2,573**

Fermanagh & Omagh **41**

Ryedale **35**

Kingston upon Hull **3,665**

Manchester **4,666**

East Lindsey **78**

King's Lynn & West Norfolk **105**

Leicester **4,772**

Birmingham **4,196**

Breckland **105**

Powys **26**

Herefordshire **87**

Luton **5,042**

Cardiff **2,564**

London **5,590**

West Somerset **47**

Chichester **150**

Portsmouth **5,371**

Bournemouth **4,297**

West Devon **47**

## OLDEST AND YOUNGEST LOCAL AUTHORITIES

When you look around your local area, what's the average age of the community? This is one of the things population estimates aim to measure using the median age of local authorities, regions and counties in the UK.

The median is one kind of average you learnt in school but may not use so often: it's the person in the middle. You could measure this in your own household: say you live with two people, the median age would be the age of the person between the oldest and the youngest. With such small numbers of people, the median age can swing quite widely, but with large populations it provides a more reliable average as it's not skewed by a few very old or very young people.

And the results? Well, they're interesting, but maybe not so surprising. Cities dominate the youngest local areas and they're often cities with universities. The university aspect obviously affects the results, although possibly not as much as you'd think because the estimates are taken on 30 June, a few weeks after most universities finish for summer. Older people tend to live in rural areas, which fits with certain stereotypes, although with an aging population it'll be interesting to see how this shifts over time.

Data from 2016 and by local authority or equivalent.

### OLDEST PLACES IN UK

| Place | Median age |
|---|---|
| West Somerset | 54.6 |
| North Norfolk | 53 |
| Rother | 52.3 |
| East Dorset | 51.7 |
| West Dorset | 51.5 |
| East Lindsey | 51.2 |
| Christchurch | 50.6 |
| South Hams | 50.6 |
| East Devon | 50.5 |
| South Lakeland | 50.3 |

### YOUNGEST PLACES IN UK

| Place | Median age |
|---|---|
| Hackney | 32.3 |
| Barking & Dagenham | 32.1 |
| Islington | 32 |
| Leicester | 31.9 |
| Cambridge | 31.3 |
| Newham | 31.1 |
| Tower Hamlets | 30.6 |
| Oxford | 30.1 |
| Nottingham | 30 |
| Manchester | 30 |

### MEDIAN AGE BY COUNTRY, 2016

| 38 | 42 | 40 | 42 |
|---|---|---|---|
|  |  |  |  |
| Northern Ireland | Scotland | England | Wales |

MEDIAN AGE OF
POPULATION

○ Oldest
○ Youngest

○ Na h-Eileanan Siar **48**

Aberdeen City **36** ○

○ Argyll & Bute **49**

Glasgow City **36** ○          ○ City of Edinburgh **36**
                              ○ West Lothian **41**

                                        ○ Northumberland **47**

Causeway Coasts & Glens **41** ○
Derry City & Strabane **37** ○          ○ Dumfries and Galloway **49**
Mid Ulster **36** ○      ○ Mid & East Antrim **42**          ○ Newcastle upon Tyne **33**
Belfast **36** ○ ○ Ards & North Down **43**

Newry, Mourne & Down **37** ○          ○ South Lakeland **50**          ○ Ryedale **50**

                              ○ Leeds **36**

                              ○ Manchester **30**          ○ East Lindsey **51**

Conwy **49** ○

                              ○ Nottingham **30**
                                        North Norfolk **53** ○
                              ○ Leicester **32**

Powys **49** ○          ○ Birmingham **33**
                    ○ Malvern Hills **50**          ○ Cambridge **31**

Monmouthshire **48** ○          ○ Oxford **30**
Swansea **40** ○      ○ Newport **39**
                    ○ Cardiff **34**          ○ London **35**
                    ○ Bristol **33**

          ○ West Somerset **55**
                    ○ East Dorset **52**          ○ Rother **52**
East Devon **51** ○      ○ Christchurch **51**
                    ○ West Dorset **52**

          ○ South Hams **51**

## POPULATION GROWTH BY NUMBERS

We often think of population growth in terms of the number of births. We might even factor immigration into the equation. But one of the biggest factors feeding into the growth in the UK's population (and the world's) is longer lives. We're used to average life expectancy increasing, but it tends to go up slowly, so the effect seems minimal. But when you multiply that increase by the population, you start to see what a massive effect this has over time.

**5,212**

The number of extra residents per square kilometre living in Tower Hamlets from 2002 to 2017

**-805**

The fall in the number of residents per square kilometre living in Kensington & Chelsea from 2002 to 2017

**762,**

**602,**

**TOTAL NUMBER OF DEATHS, UK**

**-900**

Births minus deaths for Wales (2016–2017)

**9**

Deaths per 1,000 residents in the UK from 2016–17

**-4,000**

Births minus deaths for
Scotland (2016–2017)

**157,000**

Births minus deaths
for England (2016–2017)

# 000

**TOTAL NUMBER
OF BIRTHS, UK**

# 000

## 28

The number of extra residents per
square kilometre living in the UK
from 2002 to 2017

## 12

Births per 1,000 residents in
the UK from 2016–17

**8,000**

Births minus deaths for
Northern Ireland
(2016-2017)

# BIRTHS, DEATHS AND MIGRATIONS

The three main drivers of population change are births, deaths and net international migration (those coming into the country minus those leaving). Changes to each of these have multiple factors and there are long-term trends in the UK: life expectancy has increased over time and the birth rate has fallen.

With migration flows, it's a little trickier. There's been a general increase in the number of people moving to the UK, but it's far from a straight line upwards – there was a plateau at 600,000 from 2004 to 2011, the figures dipped in 2012 and jumped back up from 2014 to 2016. Meanwhile, the figures for those leaving have stayed in

**2001**

Population change
**1,300,000**

**2004**

**2005**

Population change
**1,850,000**

**2008**

**2009**

Population change
**1,850,000**

**2012**

**2013**

Population change
**1,930,000**

**2016**

 = 100,000 international outward migration

 = 100,000 deaths

a range between 300,000 and 400,000 since 2000, only breaching 400,000 once in 2008.

These figures form a trend of net international migration, increasing the UK population every year since 1994. For many of those years, it was a significant driver: between 2001 and 2004, two-thirds of the UK's population growth was down to net immigration. And in the periods covered in this image, only in 2009 to 2012 did net immigration contribute less than half of the UK's total population increase.

Population change data rounded to the nearest 10,000 and includes a small number categorised as 'Other'.

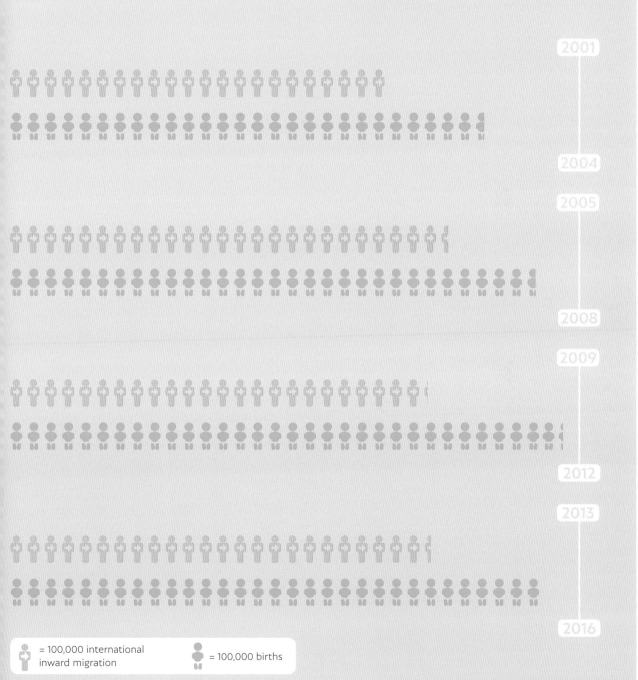

= 100,000 international inward migration

= 100,000 births

2001
2004
2005
2008
2009
2012
2013
2016

# CENTENARIANS

Did you know you can apply for the Queen to send someone a birthday card for their 100th birthday? She'll also send a card to every person reaching 105 and a card for every birthday thereafter. Just think of all those cards.

Presumably, not everyone applies, but if they did, the Queen would surely be writing birthday cards every day. By 2014, she'd have been up to about 18 cards a day – possibly writing cards to various Johns, Williams and Georges (the three most popular boys' names in 1914). But it's far more likely they're for a Mary, Margaret or Doris – women are almost six times as likely to live past 100 than men.

Although these estimates are rounded to the nearest ten, they cannot be guaranteed to be precise even to that level of detail.

MEN & WOMEN WHO LIVED TO 100 BY YEAR

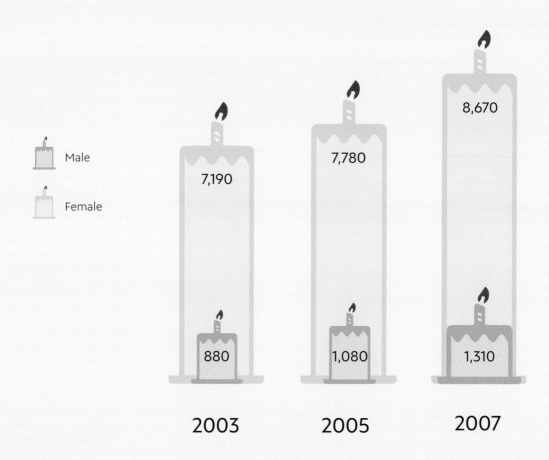

Male

Female

7,190

7,780

8,670

880

1,080

1,310

2003

2005

2007

**18**

APPROXIMATE NUMBER OF
BIRTHDAY CARDS THE
QUEEN WOULD WRITE
PER DAY

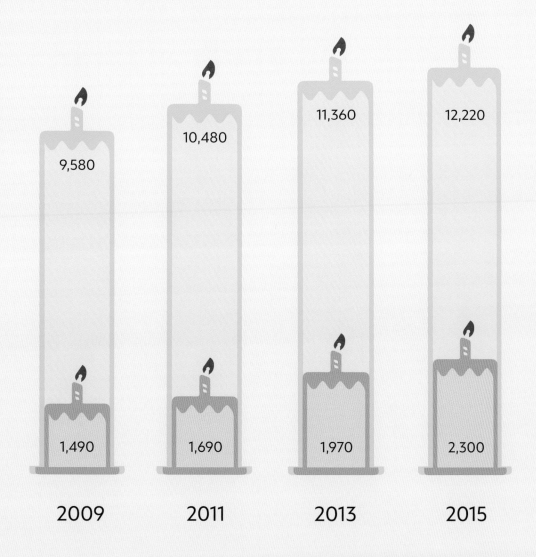

9,580

10,480

11,360

12,220

1,490

1,690

1,970

2,300

2009

2011

2013

2015

# 2

# FAMILY
# AND
# RELATIONSHIPS

# MARRIAGE

There were approximately eight marriages a year for every 1,000 people for much of the 20th century. Despite this stable number, there were bumper years around the world wars. In these bumper years (1915, 1919 and 1920 for the First World War and 1939 to 1942 for the Second World War) there were 10 marriages for every 1,000 people, although this jumped to 12 in 1940.

This number began to slide from the mid-1970s. We averaged six in the 1990s, five in the noughties and we were down to four marriages per 1,000 people in 2015, almost back to the same number of marriages as in 1890. This might reflect changes in British life and our attitudes towards marriage – and you'd expect marriage to fall in an aging population: most marriages are between young people.

But it's not looking totally glum for marriage rates: same-sex marriages were zero in 2013 and they're now on the rise.

## SAME-SEX MARRIAGES

|  | England | Wales | Scotland |
|---|---|---|---|
| 2014 | 4,620 | 230 | 370* |
| 2015 | 6,170 | 330 | 1,670 |

* Same-sex marriages came into effect in March 2014 (December 2014 in Scotland).

POPULATION
46,029,200

POPULATION
41,361,500

POPULATION
37,484,800

1890

1915

1940

ALL MARRIAGES
271,500

ALL MARRIAGES
405,000
+ 49%

ALL MARRIAGES
533,900
+ 32%

1890 population and marriage data include all of Ireland within the UK, whereas subsequent years include only Northern Ireland within the UK. 1890 population data excludes the Islands in the British Seas' populations and the Armed Forces and Merchant Service Abroad.

The 1915 civilian population includes only resident civilians, not any armed forces either posted home or abroad, although these are mid-year estimates taken before the First World War started.

## CIVIL PARTNERSHIPS BY COUNTRY

| | England | Wales | Scotland | N. Ireland |
|---|---|---|---|---|
| 2005* | 1,790 | 70 | 80 | 10 |
| 2008 | 6,280 | 280 | 530 | 90 |
| 2011 | 5,900 | 250 | 550 | 90 |
| 2014 | 1,620 | 70 | 440 | 110 |
| 2017 | 880 | 30 | 70 | 90 |

* Civil partnerships came into effect in December 2005.

84% OF GRETNA GREEN
MARRIAGES IN 2017 INVOLVED
NO SCOTTISH RESIDENTS

Includes same-sex marriages.

POPULATION
65,110,000

POPULATION
54,349,500

POPULATION
57,237,500

**1965**

**1990**

**2015**

ALL MARRIAGES
422,100
- 21%

ALL MARRIAGES
375,400
- 11%

ALL MARRIAGES
283,600
- 24%

2015 marriage data include
same-sex marriages but not
civil partnerships.

Rounded to the nearest hundred, except civil partnerships and
same-sex marriages, which are rounded to the nearest ten.

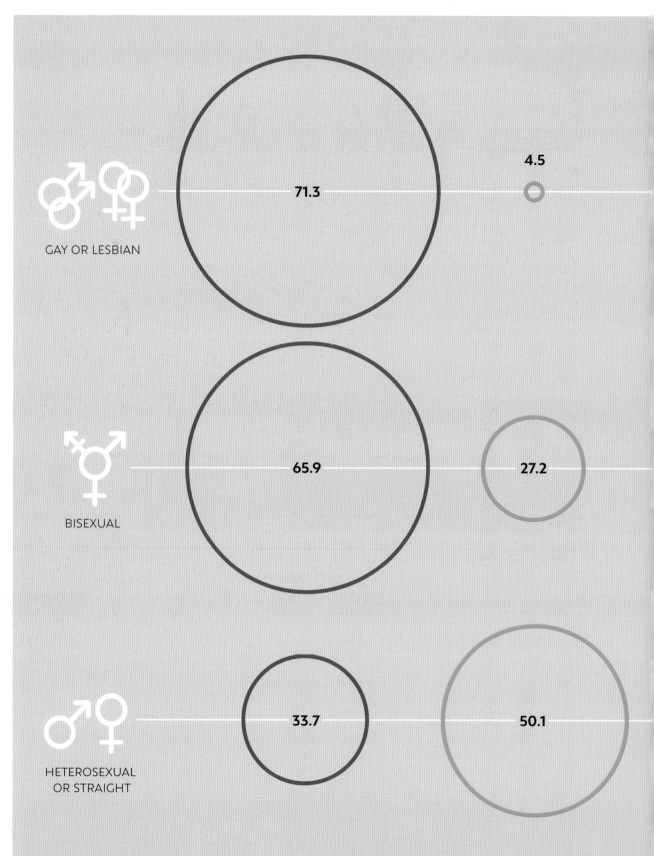

GAY OR LESBIAN

71.3

4.5

BISEXUAL

65.9

27.2

HETEROSEXUAL
OR STRAIGHT

33.7

50.1

7.9         5         0.6         10.6

## RELATIONSHIP STATUS BY SEXUALITY

Same-sex marriage has been legal since 2014 (although it's not yet recognised in Northern Ireland). Civil partnerships (which are recognised throughout the UK) were passed in 2004. In many respects, it's no surprise that a large proportion of gay and bisexual people have opted for neither – the opportunity is still relatively new. This also explains the lower rates of divorce, although not necessarily for bisexuals.

Either way, there are important stats that these figures miss: less than 3% of the population identified themselves as

0.8         4.4         0.8         0.8

non-heterosexual in 2017, although that was more than 5% for 16 to 24 year olds (1.2% for those over 65). There are also regional differences – only 1.6% of Northern Irelanders say they are non-heterosexual. Presumably, cultural differences make up some of these disparities, so if attitudes to LGBT+ continue to soften, the number of people identifying with this group should increase. The question is, will more of them get married?

Data from 2017.
* Married and civil partnership figures include couples who are separated.
** Divorced includes dissolved civil partnerships.
*** Widowed includes surviving members of a civil partnership.

0         9.1         7         0

Single (%)    Married: Opposite sex (%)*    Married: Same sex (%)*

Divorced (%)**    Widowed (%)***    Civil partnered (%)*

# CHLOE
1

# EMILY
2

# SOPHIE
3

# MEGAN
4

# REBECCA
5

# LAUREN
6

# JESSICA
7

# HANNAH
8

# CHARLOTTE
9

# AMY
10

AMELIA-ROSE WAS THE MOST POPULAR HYPHENATED FIRST NAME IN 2016; IN 1997 IT WAS JAMIE-LEE

## BABY NAMES

Baby names are fascinating. Given a list we're likely to look for our own name (there were 37 UK-born babies named Stuart in 2016, as I'm sure you were wondering). We might even feel conflicted if we're high or low on the list – is it better to be more unique or do people give babies our name because it's such a good one? Some people might make whatever argument best suits their name's position in a given year. Other people, that is – not you, dear reader.

*Continued over page* ➤

# OLIVIA 1

## AMELIA 2

## EMILY 3

## ISLA 4

## AVA 5

## JESSICA 6

## ELLA 7

## LILY 8

## SOPHIE 9

SOPHIA 10

HARPER
THERE WERE
BARELY ANY BABIES
NAMED HARPER IN
1997; IN 2016 THERE
WERE MORE
THAN 1,400

EMMA
MADE THE
TOP FIVE IN
SCOTLAND AND
NORTHERN IRELAND
IN 1997

## 1997

1. JACK
2. JAMES
3. THOMAS
4. DANIEL
5. MATTHEW
6. JOSHUA
7. RYAN
8. SAMUEL
9. JORDAN
10. JOSEPH

BECKHAM
THERE WERE A SMALL
NUMBER OF BABIES
NAMED BECKHAM
IN 1997, BUT NONE
REPORTED
IN 2016

But baby names give us other insights: famous people with unique names and even television characters appear on the list at the time when they are popular (not too many 'Cersei's, oddly enough, but four 'Daenery's in 2016, the year the sixth season of *Game of Thrones* premiered). And because this kind of data is high quality (it's easy to count baby names when births are registered), there's a lot of data on less common names.

# OLIVER 1
## 2016
# HARRY 2
# JACK 3
# GEORGE 4
# JACOB 5
# NOAH 6
# CHARLIE 7
# JAMES 8
# THOMAS 9
## OSCAR 10

JACK, JAMES & OLIVER MADE THE TOP THREE FOR BOTH SCOTLAND AND NORTHERN IRELAND IN 2016

MOHAMMED FIRST APPEARED IN THE TOP 100 BABY NAMES FOR BOYS BORN IN ENGLAND AND WALES IN 1924

And then there's the politics of spelling: 'Mohammed' and its various spellings often make news stories debating whether it's the most popular name this year. Although the same could be said for any number of names – Sophie and Sophy, for example. The official list counts each spelling as a different name and lets the public think what they want.

# LIVE BIRTHS

In the 1990s, there were news stories about early-teenage pregnancies. And in the noughties, older mothers caught the headlines. Yet neither are unique: the decade that saw the most teenagers becoming mothers was easily the 1960s, reaching a peak in 1966. The number of teenagers giving birth has been trending downwards ever since. As for those over 40 giving birth, the numbers have been creeping upwards for some time, but they are still below 1945 levels – I guess soldiers returned after the Second World War and celebrations followed...

**994,000**
**1947**
MOST BIRTHS
IN ONE YEAR
ALL AGES

**658,000**
**1977**
LEAST BIRTHS
IN ONE YEAR
ALL AGES

## LIVE BIRTHS
## TEENS vs OVER-40s

Rounded to the nearest thousand.

### Teens (under 20)

**1950s**
**398,000**

**1960s**
**824,000**

**1970s**
**766,000**

**1980s**
**652,000**

**1990s**
**538,000**

**2000s**
**503,000**

### Over-40s

**1950s**
**256,000**

**1960s**
**235,000**

**1970s**
**99,000**

**1980s**
**87,000**

**1990s**
**128,000**

**2000s**
**237,000**

**96,000**
**1966 TEENS**
MOST BIRTHS
IN ONE YEAR

**7,000**
**1977 OVER-40s**
LEAST BIRTHS
IN ONE YEAR

# LIVE BIRTHS BY DECADE

**1950s**
7.93m

**1960s**
9.32m

**1970s**
7.43m

**1980s**
7.5m

**1990s**
7.49m

**2000s**
7.26m

## BABY BOOM OR BABY POP

All those teenagers having babies in the 1960s definitely contributed to the baby boom. But how many children make a baby boom? There were 9.3 million children born in the 1960s, but a boom is likely a proportional thing: a large number of kids to adults. After all, there were only 1.5 million more babies born in the 1960s than in the 1950s – 1.5 million additional babies over 10 years seems less like a boom and more like a pop.

In the 1961 Census, there were 52.7 million people in the UK. Now the UK has topped 65.5 million and in the noughties there were 7.3 million new arrivals – 2 million fewer than in the 1960s. To get to the same proportion of kids to adults as the 1960s we might need more than 4 million additional kids birthed this decade over the last one. Or maybe an additional 1.5 million littl'uns is enough for another baby pop.

Due to data availability, Northern Ireland data are only included from 1976 and annual data from 1976 to 1990 are only published as annual averages over a five-year period.

# BIRTHS OUTSIDE OF MARRIAGE

Data is amoral. It does not say whether it's better to be married when you have kids. Including this graph in the book might suggest a leaning towards traditional principles, but the author has a child out of wedlock and the truth is we probably all know people with similar family set-ups. And it's certainly true from the data that the number of children born to unmarried parents has been steadily increasing since the 1970s (for England and Wales at least – data starts a little later for Scotland and Northern Ireland). Yet morals aside, the data are still interesting: the prevalence of births outside of marriage varies quite widely across regions.

The reasons for these divergences are sometimes unclear. Do religion or traditional values play a role in Northern Ireland? If so, does that apply to the South East or the East of England, which both have similar levels of births outside of marriage? And where does London sit in all this?

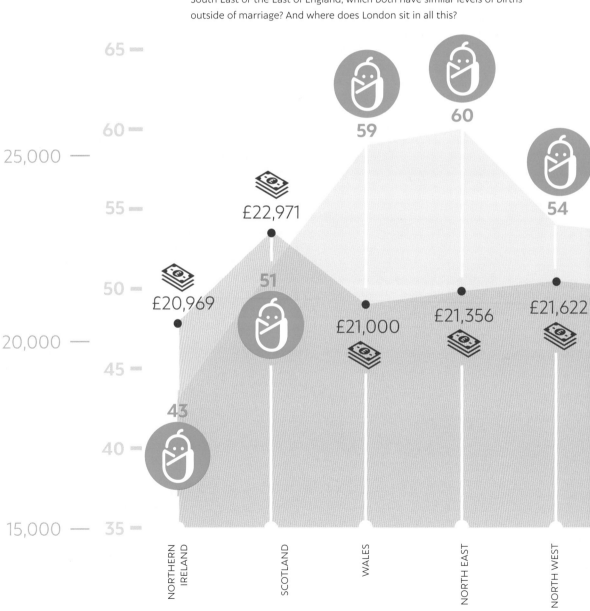

£

%

30,000 — 70 —

65 —

60 —    59      60

25,000 —

55 —    £22,971      54

50 — £20,969   51     £21,356   £21,622

£21,000

20,000 —

45 —

43

40 —

15,000 — 35 —

NORTHERN IRELAND    SCOTLAND    WALES    NORTH EAST    NORTH WEST

The 2011 Census provides detailed information on the number of unmarried households with children, providing a snapshot at one period of time, versus the births to unmarried couples for one year as shown on this page. Census data show regional similarities: across the UK around 1 in 20 households have an unmarried couple with at least one dependent child. The figures are a little higher for lone parents, although it's here where London and Northern Ireland stand out again: in London, dependent children in unmarried households are twice as likely to live with a lone parent than with an unmarried couple – they're more than three times as likely in Northern Ireland.

Snapshots are important, but situations can change: people with children get married, for example. Similarly, family arrangements for the birth cohort in any given year can change. Understanding these shifts from a national perspective is an ongoing and fascinating endeavour.

Data from 2016.

UK-WIDE FIGURES
**£23,084**
Median wage

**48%**
Births outside of marriage

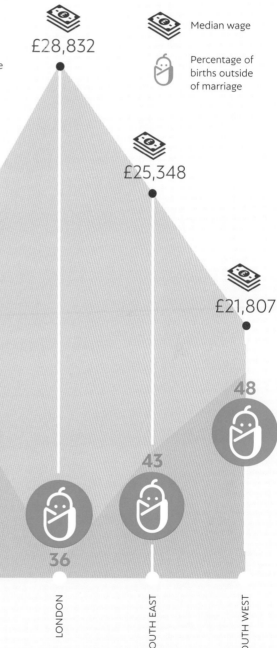

Median wage

Percentage of births outside of marriage

£28,832

£25,348

£24,218

£21,789

£21,807

53

52

£21,790

£21,251

50

46

48

36

43

YORKSHIRE & THE HUMBER

EAST MIDLANDS

WEST MIDLANDS

EAST OF ENGLAND

LONDON

SOUTH EAST

SOUTH WEST

# SPENDING ON LITTLE ONES

Having kids is expensive. And according to these data, almost 3 out of every 5 pounds spent on kids goes on clothes and childcare. That is, of course, if you exclude all the things you buy for kids that you'd also buy for adults: food, transport, entry tickets for days out...

Figures represent average annual household expenditure, 2016/17. Kids' clothes and kids' footwear are for children under 16.

CHILDCARE
PAYMENTS
£125

PRAMS,
PUSHCHAIRS
& ACCESSORIES
£10

BABY
EQUIPMENT
(excluding prams
& pushchairs)
£10

KIDS' CLOTHES
£157

NURSERY, CRÈCHE
& PLAYSCHOOLS
£52

KIDS' FOOTWEAR
£42

**6,166**

NO CHILDREN

**1,982**
ONE CHILD

**1,782**
NO CHILDREN

**642**
ONE CHILD

○ Married couple

○ Opposite sex cohabiting couple family

● Lone parent

Figures are in thousands.

**972**
ONE CHILD

# FAMILY TYPES

No matter the subject, data requires categories so that we can aggregate and interpret. But categories ignore nuance. These data come from a household survey and they provide our best estimates. Yet where should we put someone with kids from a previous relationship, but no kids with their current partner? If the kids don't live with them, then they could fall into 'no children', which is misleading, and the details of their situation are impossible to see in the data.

Data from 2017. Excludes those who state they 'only have non-dependent children' – see Notes for definition of non-dependent children.

——— 2,156 ———
TWO CHILDREN

— 806 —
THREE OR MORE
CHILDREN

— 438 —
TWO CHILDREN

— 166 —
THREE OR MORE
CHILDREN

— 585 —
TWO CHILDREN

— 224 —
THREE OR MORE
CHILDREN

# LIVING ARRANGEMENTS

Do you know anyone who likes the taste of their mother's cooking just a bit too much? When did they leave home? Although more than half of men move out by their early 20s, more than 1 in 10 are still at home in their early 30s. The number is less than 1 in 20 for women, although they tend to still be at home in their early 20s.

And there has been a general trend over a couple of decades of people staying at home longer – no doubt, house prices are affecting their decisions. The age group bucking this trend are teens: young men aged between 15 and 19 were more likely to flee the nest in 2017 than 20 years earlier, although not women.

When youngsters do gain their independence, it's women who are more likely to live alone – although the difference between men and women has narrowed significantly between 1996 and 2017. This narrowing has been driven by men over 45 – those under 45 were less likely to live alone than they were in the mid-1990s. Part of this could be generational: men living alone in the 1990s have grown older, assuming their living situation has remained stable. The other part of the trend I'll leave to researchers. Or those armchair speculators holding an infographic book full of UK data.

Notes
• The term 'parent' could include grandparents, step-parents or foster parents.
• Once a person lives with a partner or has a child, they are considered to have formed their own family and are deemed to be not living with their parents, even if they still live in the same household as their parents.
• Students living in halls of residence during term-time and living with their parents outside term-time are counted as not living with their parents.

LIVING WITH PARENTS
FEMALE TO MALE RATIO, 2017

Age 15–19

Age 20–24

Age 25–29

Age 30–34

# LIVING ALONE, AGED 45 AND OVER

## DIVORCE

Divorce is a messy business. More than 110,000 UK couples went through it in 2015 with 2 out of 5 saying their partner behaved unreasonably. That's more than 200,000 people affected by divorce in a single year – and for more than 38,000 of them, it was not their first split.

The data on how long marriages last are interesting: a small proportion of couples decide quickly that they made the wrong choice. By 20 years, three-quarters of all divorces have occurred. But that's assuming these proportions remain stable over time, which isn't always the case. In England and Wales, divorce rates actually reached a peak in 1993 at 14 marriages in every 1,000 ending in divorce. They remained relatively elevated after that but have been on a downward trend since 2008. In 2017, 8 marriages for every 1,000 ended in divorce.

I've been married for 10 years this year* and although divorce is less likely to separate a couple than death, these data make me think I shouldn't drop my guard. My wife's had her eye on Colin Firth for some time now.

* My wife corrected me: it's nine years this year.

DIVORCE BY REASON, 2015

| 12,000 | 48,000 | 29,000 | 21,000 |
|---|---|---|---|
| Adultery | Unreasonable behaviour | Living apart and consenting to divorce | Living apart and one party does not consent |

In Scotland a person can divorce if they have led 'separate lives' for one year and they both agree to the divorce. If one of the partners disagrees then they must live separate lives for two years. There were similar rules in the rest of the UK in 2015, but the equivalent time periods were two and five years, respectively.
Figures rounded to the nearest thousand.

DIVORCE BY AGE, 2015

| | | |
|---|---|---|
| NOT KNOWN | 8% | 8% |
| 60+ | 6% | 9% |
| 50–59 | 19% | 23% |
| 40–49 | 32% | 33% |
| 30–39 | 27% | 23% |
| LESS THAN 30 | 8% | 5% |

YEARS

| | |
|---|---|
| NOT STATED | 9% |
| 30+ | 7% |
| 25–29 | 7% |
| 20–24 | 10% |
| 15–19 | 12% |
| 10–14 | 18% |
| 5–9 | 23% |
| 0–4 | 14% |

DURATION OF MARRIAGE AT TIME
OF DIVORCE, 2015

England and Wales duration data for more than 15 years are
based on author calculations – see Notes for more details.

# 3

# HOUSE AND HOME

# WHO BUILDS BRITAIN?

In post-war Britain the state led a significant portion of the nation's rebuilding efforts. And these efforts were spearheaded by local authorities, which were responsible for the vast majority of new houses in the UK. A lot has happened since and the private sector is now the dominant builder in Britain, with housing associations playing a notable part.

Yet the number of houses built in the UK has fallen considerably over the decades. This is a complicated story and there are several factors. It could be argued that we need less housing now: in the 1940s and 1950s we needed to replace bombed housing stock, in the 1960s we had a baby boom and now we have that housing stock, it's not so necessary to build as many houses as we did in those decades.

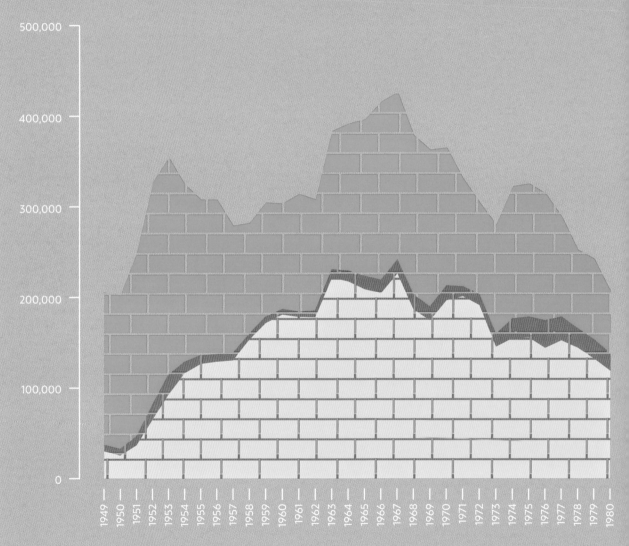

But high house prices suggest the demand for housing outstrips supply.

Some will argue that local authorities need to return to the business of building houses, while others will say that planning permissions are too strict, preventing private companies from building more. What is clear is that housing is, and will remain, a key issue in UK politics for the foreseeable future and who builds Britain in the future might be up for grabs.

Notes
• These figures are for new build dwellings only.
• Northern Ireland data prior to 2005 is sourced from the Department of Communities which uses different definitions and adjusts its data differently.
• Figures from October 2005 to March 2007 in England are missing a small number of completions that were inspected by independent approved inspectors. These data are included from June 2007.

 LOCAL AUTHORITIES

 HOUSING ASSOCIATIONS

 PRIVATE ENTERPRISE

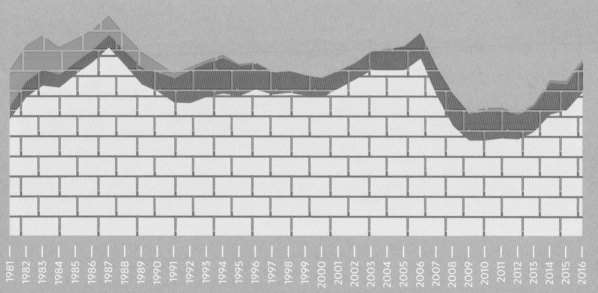

1981 1982 1983 1984 1985 1986 1987 1988 1989 1990 1991 1992 1993 1994 1995 1996 1997 1998 1999 2000 2001 2002 2003 2004 2005 2006 2007 2008 2009 2010 2011 2012 2013 2014 2015 2016

# BIGGEST CHANGES
## IN AVERAGE UK HOUSE PRICES

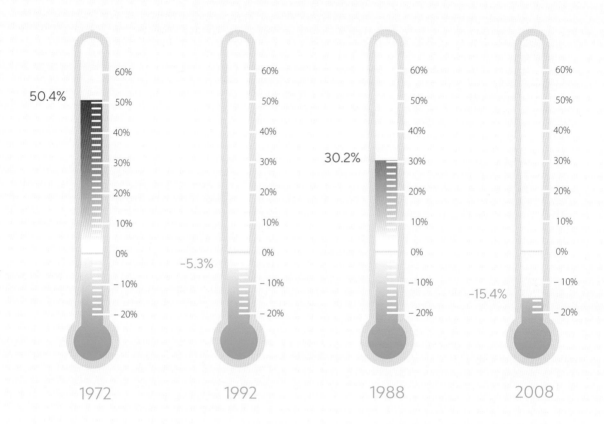

## HOUSE PRICE GROWTH

We've all heard that house prices have grown incredibly fast recently, but how does this compare with other periods in UK history? The fact is that average house price growth was highest in the 1970s. Yet this was from a low base: for example, moving from £10,000 to £20,000 is a jump of 100%, but if you start at £100,000, then a 10% jump will provide the same increase in the overall price.

More recent increases are smaller in percentage terms, but they've had a much larger effect. Furthermore, as prices have risen faster, they have seen more damaging falls: 2008 saw the largest fall in house prices since the UK began collecting data

on average house prices in 1969. The average value of a house fell almost 15.5% – far more than the second worst year (down 5.3% in 1992).

In general, like many markets, prices in housing tend to go up. This is partly due to inflation, although interactions between housing supply, population and changes to living arrangements will all have an effect. Put this together and house price falls have been historically rare. Since 1969, year-on-year house prices have grown 86% of the time. Yet, as recent increases have been so large, the big question is whether we'll see more volatile house prices in future. It's certainly a risk.

Annual (or decade) average house price growth is based on the growth between 1st January of the (first) year being measured and 1st January of the following year (or decade).

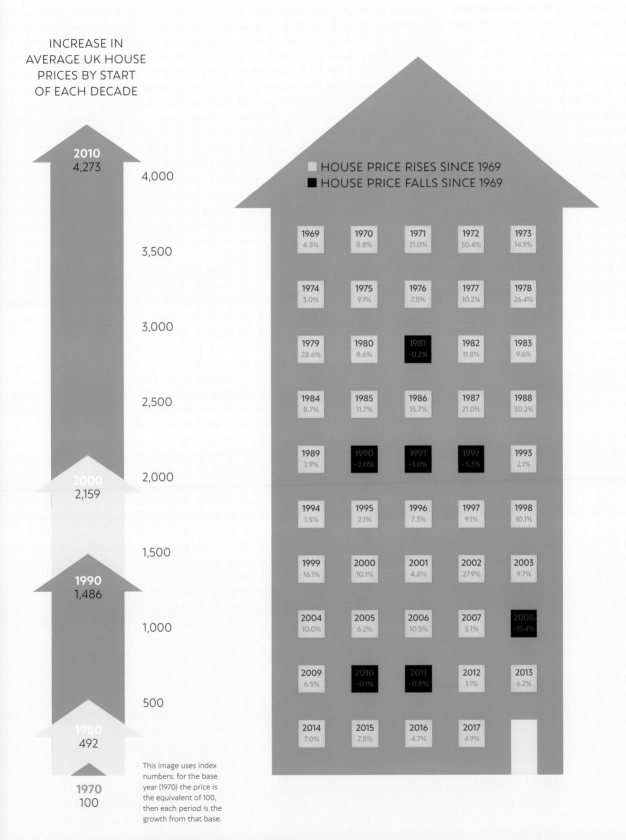

INCREASE IN AVERAGE UK HOUSE PRICES BY START OF EACH DECADE

2010
4,273

2000
2,159

1990
1,486

1980
492

1970
100

4,000

3,500

3,000

2,500

2,000

1,500

1,000

500

This image uses index numbers: for the base year (1970) the price is the equivalent of 100, then each period is the growth from that base.

■ HOUSE PRICE RISES SINCE 1969
■ HOUSE PRICE FALLS SINCE 1969

| 1969 4.3% | 1970 8.8% | 1971 21.0% | 1972 50.4% | 1973 14.9% |
| 1974 3.0% | 1975 9.1% | 1976 7.5% | 1977 10.2% | 1978 26.4% |
| 1979 28.6% | 1980 8.6% | 1981 -0.2% | 1982 11.8% | 1983 9.6% |
| 1984 8.7% | 1985 11.7% | 1986 15.7% | 1987 21.0% | 1988 30.2% |
| 1989 2.9% | 1990 -2.0% | 1991 -1.0% | 1992 -5.3% | 1993 2.1% |
| 1994 1.5% | 1995 2.1% | 1996 7.3% | 1997 9.1% | 1998 10.1% |
| 1999 16.1% | 2000 10.1% | 2001 4.8% | 2002 27.9% | 2003 9.7% |
| 2004 10.0% | 2005 6.2% | 2006 10.5% | 2007 5.1% | 2008 -15.4% |
| 2009 6.5% | 2010 -0.1% | 2011 -0.8% | 2012 1.1% | 2013 6.2% |
| 2014 7.0% | 2015 7.8% | 2016 4.7% | 2017 4.9% | |

# HOUSE PRICE CHANGES

With house price statistics often pointing upwards (watch out for 'slowdown in growth' headlines – still growing, but at a slower rate), it's easy to forget regional differences. Over the 13 years covered by these data, some places saw relatively subdued increases. On a country level, only house prices in Scotland and England beat house-price-inflation. Of course, this is only true when measuring point-to-point, ignoring the boom in between, but few (if any) of us trade houses in the way an investor trades shares, hoping to take advantage of peaks and troughs.

DID YOU KNOW?
HOUSE PRICES IN THE UK HAVE RISEN BY 6,000% SINCE THE BEATLES RELEASED THE WHITE ALBUM

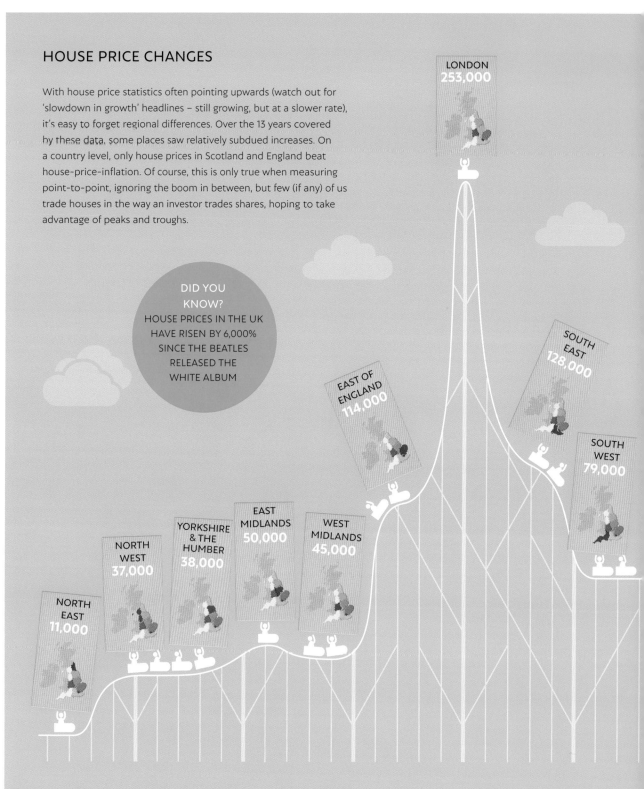

LONDON
253,000

SOUTH EAST
128,000

SOUTH WEST
79,000

EAST OF ENGLAND
114,000

EAST MIDLANDS
50,000

WEST MIDLANDS
45,000

YORKSHIRE & THE HUMBER
38,000

NORTH WEST
37,000

NORTH EAST
11,000

AVERAGE HOUSE PRICE CHANGE BY REGION

Only three regions (plus Scotland) beat inflation or the UK average: London, the South East, and East of England. The South West came close, but the increase in value was on already high prices, so the rate of change was not quite good enough to make it a star performer. Of the high-performing regions, London is leading the charge. And the extent to which London has surged ahead is significant.

On the other end of the scale, house price growth in the North West is 40 percentage points below growth in the UK (50% house price growth versus just 10% for the North West). This is a far cry from London's heady increase of almost 110%.

Figures rounded to the nearest thousand.

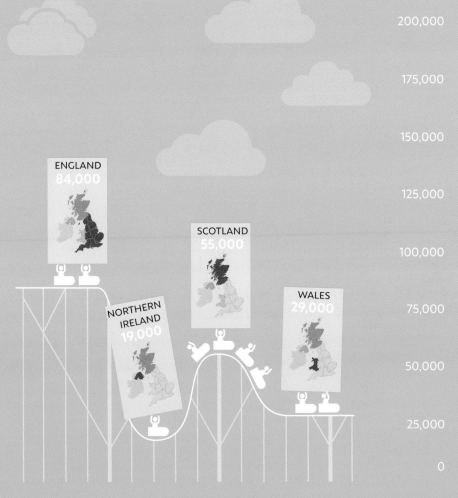

£

250,000

225,000

200,000

175,000

150,000

125,000

100,000

75,000

50,000

25,000

0

ENGLAND
84,000

SCOTLAND
55,000

NORTHERN
IRELAND
19,000

WALES
29,000

AVERAGE HOUSE PRICE CHANGE BY COUNTRY

## 2005

£427,968

£114,567

1 CHELSEA FLAT COULD BUY 3.7 DETACHED BURNLEY HOUSES

## 2018

£1,212,590

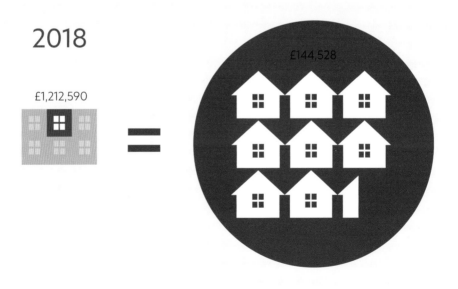

£144,528

1 CHELSEA FLAT COULD BUY 8.4 DETACHED BURNLEY HOUSES

# THE POWER OF CHELSEA

If it's all about location location location, then for the recent past, it's been all about Chelsea Chelsea Chelsea.

As a local authority, Kensington & Chelsea has had the most expensive average house price in the UK* every month since the beginning of 2005. This is pretty much true for every property type – flat, terrace, semi-detached and detached properties.** Furthermore, Kensington & Chelsea saw the fastest growth in property prices from January 2005 to January 2018. This is quite remarkable, when you consider how the maths work: if you start at a low base, say £20,000 for a property, and local prices increase by £60,000, then that home is now three times more expensive. If you start at a higher base of closer to £500,000, as Chelsea did, then the value of that home would have to increase by £1 million to reach the same percentage growth.

On the other end of the scale, the house price boom has certainly missed some areas. The top spot for cheapest houses was passed from region to region over the period covered in these data. As we entered 2005, the Shetland Islands had the cheapest detached houses in Great Britain (there are no data by property type for this period for Northern Ireland), while Wrexham had the cheapest semi-detached and terrace houses, and Merthyr Tydfil in Wales had the lowest priced flats. Merthyr Tydfil and Wrexham retained their spots as we entered 2018, although Na h-Eileanan Siar in the Outer Hebrides had the cheapest detached houses by that time.

If we switch to the average house price for all property types, then Burnley had the lowest prices in the UK (including Northern Ireland) at the start of 2005 and the start of 2018. Meanwhile, the area that grew the slowest was County Durham. The average property in January 2005 was worth just £2,000 more in January 2018.

It is tempting to put these differences down to house price falls following the financial crisis in 2008. But the average house price in Chelsea dropped 28% from local area peak to trough,*** which was a much larger fall than for County Durham (17.5% fall in local peak to trough) and a little more than Burnley (26.5%). And Chelsea maintained the highest average house price in the UK throughout the downturn.

* Unfortunately, we don't have house price data for property type for Northern Irish local areas or the Isles of Scilly. Although it's a pretty safe bet that Chelsea retains the highest prices in the UK.
** Camden claimed the top spot for detached houses in March 2009. Other than that, it's all Kensington & Chelsea.
*** This relates to the highest average house price for the local area prior to the downturn, then the lowest average price for the area after that downturn. These periods differ for each location and from the peak to trough for the UK as a whole.

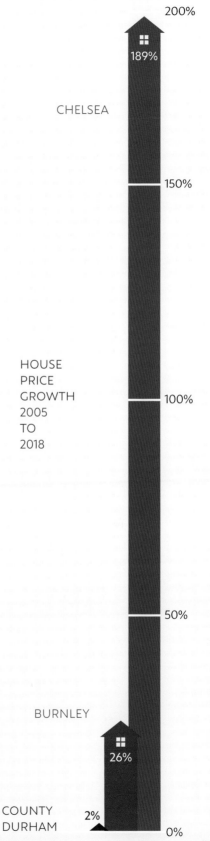

200%

CHELSEA

189%

150%

HOUSE
PRICE
GROWTH
2005
TO
2018

100%

50%

BURNLEY

26%

COUNTY
DURHAM          2%

0%

# THE HOUSING LADDER

As house prices have grown, those priced out of owning are moving to the rental sector, which has both private and social providers. But the big increase in the rented housing supply has been in the private renting market (housing associations have also grown notably on the social renting side in recent years but these have replaced falling levels of local authority housing).

This has led to a secondary effect, which is a change in tenure in a property. Private renters tend to have significantly shorter tenancies than home owners and social renters. Part of this is likely to be flexibility demanded by private renters – students, for example, may only want to rent in term time. But part of it is also likely to be reduced security for renters.

\* Social renting includes housing associations, local authority housing and other housing provided socially.

Owner occupiers

Social renters*

Private renters

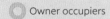

Owner occupiers

Social renters*

Private renters

LENGTH OF TENURE, 2016/17

LESS THAN 3 YEARS

HOUSING LADDERS

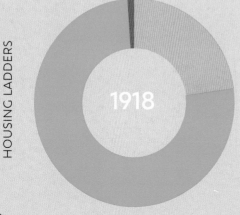

1918

1980

1918 data for England only.

64

43

34

29

22

10

3–10

MORE THAN 10 YEARS

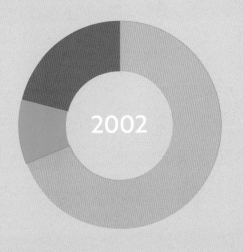

2002

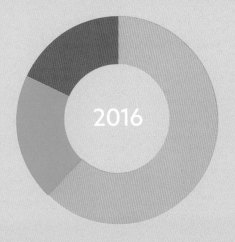

2016

73

# OWNERS AND RENTERS

Between the financial year 2006/07 and 2016/17 we had a financial crisis that hit house prices. Since those falls, house prices have recovered (although the recovery is uneven across the UK), but the proportions of home tenure have shifted markedly.

These data partly reflect an aging population, where older generations are paying off their mortgages in greater numbers; they partly reflect how high house prices make it difficult to get on the housing ladder, pushing people into renting; and they partly reflect the growth of buy-to-let trends which started before 2006, but have since grown. There's probably also a dose of those who lost their homes in the financial crisis and were still renting almost 10 years later.

20%

17%

28%

2016/17

34%

Owned outright

Buying with a mortgage

Social renting sector*

Private renting sector

* Social renting sector refers to those who rent from the
council or a housing association.

## MORTGAGE AND RENTING COSTS

Just as house prices are unevenly distributed across the UK, so are housing costs. Social housing (renting from councils or housing associations) is cheaper in Scotland than anywhere else, yet social renting aside, Northern Ireland has the cheapest housing costs in the UK.

These differences might sometimes appear small, but they are on a weekly basis. The £24 difference between social renting in Scotland and England turns into more than £1,200 a year. The difference jumps to £6,600 for those living in London.

These prices are often driven by employment, as a thriving job market will push up the demand for housing in a particular area. There are other factors that play a part – we all want to live in a good location,

WEEKLY COSTS, 2016/17

SOCIAL RENTING*

PRIVATE RENTING

family ties matter, retirees have no commute, some can work from home, rich people can pretty much buy anywhere (hello penthouse in London)... but for most of us, if we can't get to work from a particular location, we can't live there.

Yet an important element of these data is that mortgages are more expensive than private renting in every country in the UK. This is not true of every region: in England, the North East, West Midlands and South West have higher renting costs than mortgages. Even so, because owning a home comes with maintenance costs that could be high and unexpected, renting might seem like a safe option for some. Until the landlord raises the rent, that is.

£142

£115

£120

£110

MORTGAGES**

England

Wales

Scotland

Northern Ireland

* Social renting refers to those who rent from the council or a housing association.
** Only includes mortgages where both a capital payment and an interest payment are made each month – for example, interest-only mortgages are excluded.

# HOME OWNERSHIP

We should all be aware that house price growth has made it more difficult for younger people to get on the ladder while benefiting those who already own – and home ownership is more common in older age groups. But there are other dimensions of housing that we look at a little less.

Average price growth can be skewed by particularly popular areas and, as noted elsewhere in this book, London has been a hot market for some time. Because London is a relatively young city, this has led to low levels of ownership in the capital – far less than the UK as a whole. And because London is so big (about 13% of the entire population lives there), this has an outsized effect on rates of ownership among young people. It's obviously not the whole story, but it's an important part.

Then there's ethnicity. A higher proportion of white people own compared with almost any other ethnicity. This makes sense when you consider older people are more likely to be white as immigrants tend to be younger than the average UK citizen and rates of immigration have increased relatively recently. But it's possible there are other factors at play, including opportunities and family situation (the bank of mum and dad is an important element of the British housing market these days).

Yet the rate of ownership is even higher for Indians. And although Indians, Pakistanis and Bangladeshis all come from the Indian sub-continent (it was all one country when my father was born), the rates of ownership, private renting and social renting between these groups are starkly different.

On the other end of the scale, almost half of all Chinese people are private renters. These figures are high for other Asian ethnicities, but they fall significantly for Bangladeshis who are more likely to be social renters than in the private sector.

Without more details, it is hard to determine why certain groups have fallen into these living arrangements while others have taken a different path. But it's only by gathering information on these dynamics that we can better understand what life is like for different groups of people in the UK.

## HOME OWNERSHIP PROPORTIONS, 2016–17

## PERCENTAGE OF OWNERS BY AGE, 2006–07 & 2016–17

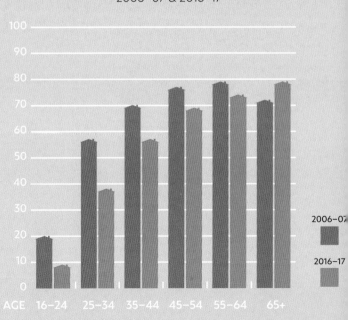

# PERCENTAGE OF HOUSEHOLDS BY TENURE
## & ETHNIC GROUP* OF HEAD, AVERAGE OF 2014–17

Owners

Social renters

Private renters

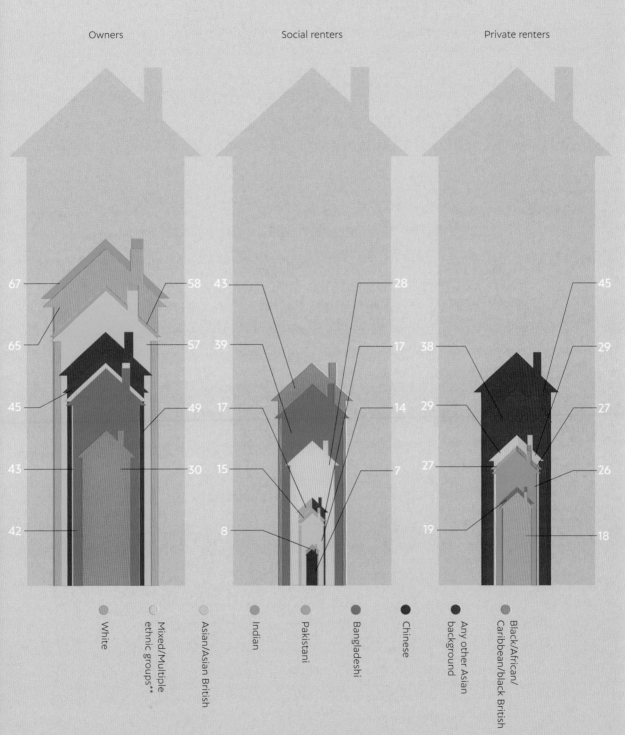

67  —  58      43  —  28                45

65  —  57      39  —  17      38        29

45  —  49      17  —  14      29        27

43  —  30      15  —  7       27        26

42            8              19         18

White

Mixed/Multiple
ethnic groups**

Asian/Asian British

Indian

Pakistani

Bangladeshi

Chinese

Any other Asian
background

Black/African/
Caribbean/black British

* Ethnicity data are averaged over three years to account for small sample sizes for some ethnic groups.
** Mixed ethnic group data represent those family backgrounds that fall into more than one ethnic
group. Due to small samples, it is not possible to disaggregate black, African, Caribbean, and black British
into seperate groups.

# 4

# EDUCATION AND EMPLOYMENT

# EDUCATION LEVELS

Those entering the workforce 45 years ago were in a different world. There were more manufacturing and production jobs, the mines were still big employers, finance was yet to be deregulated. Even 30 years ago, in the late 1980s, although things had changed, the shifts to the world today were in their infancy. So it's understandable that the qualifications required for older generations were different.

It's difficult to know whether changes in qualifications have driven changes to our job market and economy or the other way around. But the changes are

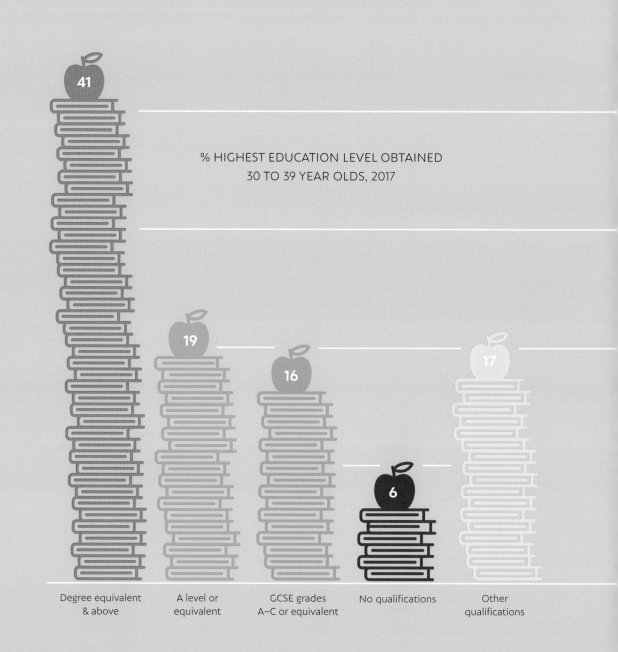

% HIGHEST EDUCATION LEVEL OBTAINED
30 TO 39 YEAR OLDS, 2017

41

19

16

6

17

Degree equivalent
& above

A level or
equivalent

GCSE grades
A–C or equivalent

No qualifications

Other
qualifications

notable – degrees have become the go-to qualification and for some jobs a bachelor's is no longer enough to distinguish yourself.

If AI predictions are correct, then machines might replace a lot of cognitive tasks, making manual skills more necessary. If that is the case, there's a question around what all these highly educated people will do.

% HIGHEST EDUCATION LEVEL OBTAINED
50 TO 64 YEAR OLDS, 2017

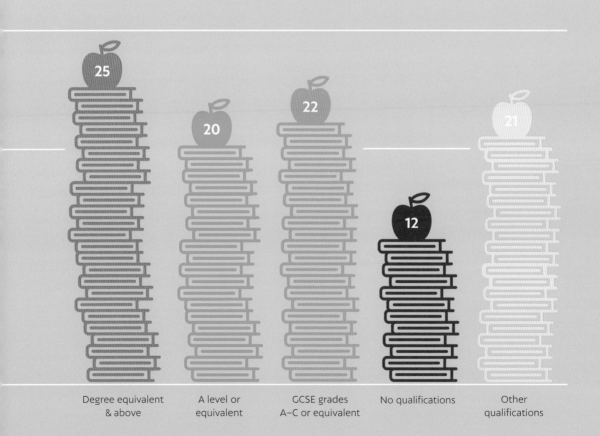

| Degree equivalent & above | A level or equivalent | GCSE grades A–C or equivalent | No qualifications | Other qualifications |

## TOP 10 SUBJECT AREAS
## FOR FIRST YEAR STUDENTS, 2015/16

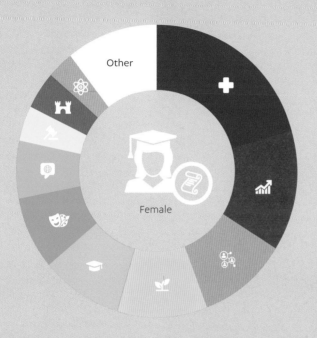

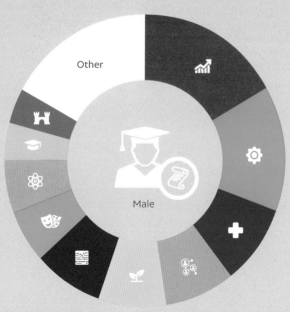

Combines undergraduate and
postgraduate for both part-time
and full-time students.

# HIGHER EDUCATION

There were more women than men enrolled in UK universities in the 2015/16 academic year. And based on this cohort, these women are likely to become our doctors and teachers, to notably increase female representation among lawyers and are more likely to be multilingual.

This trend is whisking away old-fashioned notions of a 'fairer sex' and, on the campus at least, should be indicative of a fairer playing field. Once these women have secured their qualifications, they may well play a part in tackling persistent gender pay gaps by challenging their peers in various fields.

Yet there are some subjects where men continue to hold strong majorities. These include engineering, computer science, architecture and mathematics. It seems that women entering university continue to be put off by these subjects. Is it the maths? This seems like a shoddy explanation – statistics play a significant part in several other degrees. Just ask a social scientist (of which 63% were women in 2015/16 enrolments).

There is more going on with these trends and solving this issue would be beneficial for academia and for us all: study after study shows that diversity improves our attainment, so we should all root for the 17% of female engineers and computer scientists in the 2015/16 cohort. They could be in a better place than most to change the world.

SUBJECT POPULARITY, BACHELORS & BEYOND, 2015/16

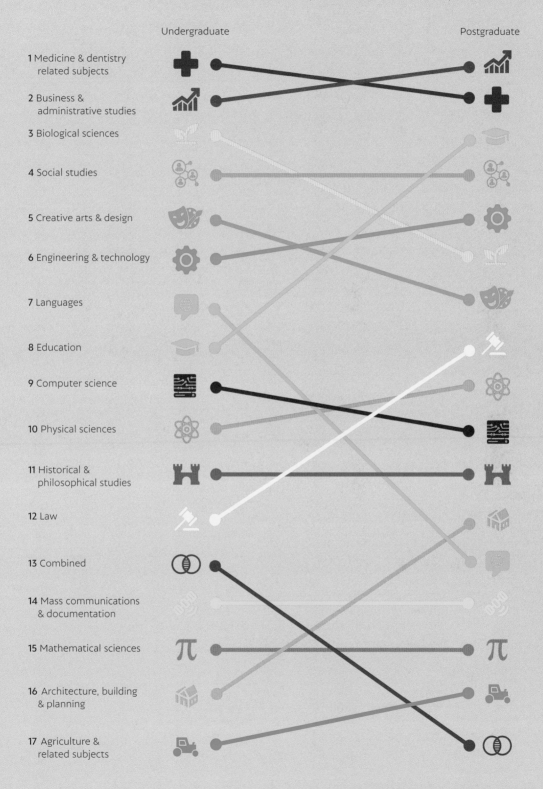

Undergraduate

Postgraduate

1 Medicine & dentistry
related subjects

2 Business &
administrative studies

3 Biological sciences

4 Social studies

5 Creative arts & design

6 Engineering & technology

7 Languages

8 Education

9 Computer science

10 Physical sciences

11 Historical &
philosophical studies

12 Law

13 Combined

14 Mass communications
& documentation

15 Mathematical sciences

16 Architecture, building
& planning

17 Agriculture &
related subjects

# FOREIGN STUDENTS

Foreign students are a boon to universities as they pay higher tuition fees. And those living in towns and cities with universities are aware that they make up a larger part of the student population than they did in the past. Yet few of us know the details of how many foreign students are in the UK, how that relates to UK students, or where they come from.

The answers to these numbers are pretty interesting: around 1 in 5 students coming to the UK to start a degree (undergrad and postgrad) in 2015 was a foreign citizen. Non-EU citizens make up more than half

of that figure. Less than 1 in 10 foreign students study part time and most of them (238,000 in 2015/16) are undergrads, although there are also a large number of postgrads (200,000). A fifth of foreign students come from China (excluding Hong Kong) and the top nine nationalities of foreign students in the UK make up 50% of the total. Despite there being fewer postgrads, non-UK citizens represent almost 2 out of every 5 postgrad students in the UK versus around 1 in 7 for undergrads. And of the institutions that have the highest proportion of foreign students, 8 out of the top 10 are in London.

## % FOREIGN STUDENTS BY NATIONALITY, 2015/16

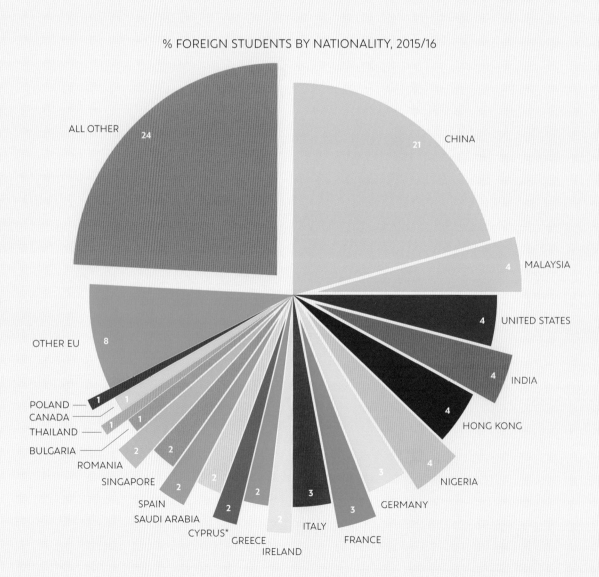

* 'Cyprus' includes students whose domicile is recorded as 'Cyprus (European Union)' or 'Cyprus not otherwise specified'.

# MOST FOREIGN STUDENTS
The UK universities with the highest foreign student enrolments in 2015/16

47 **7** 53

53 **4** 47

46 **8** 54

48 **6** 52

70 **1** 30

66 **2** 34

57 **3** 43

50 **5** 50

46 **9** 54

45 **10** 55

**AVERAGE FOREIGN STUDENTS**

Non-UK 19%

UK 81%

1. London Business School
2. London School of Economics & Political Science
3. Royal College of Art
4. Cranfield University
5. Imperial College of Science, Technology & Medicine
6. Royal College of Music
7. University of St Andrews
8. University of the Arts London
9. London School of Hygiene & Tropical Medicine
10. School of Oriental & African Studies

# JOBS BY NUMBERS

As workers, we tend to operate within a small slice of the UK's labour market. Then we hear different stories from the media. But these views can distort the actual picture. Zero-hour contracts are controversial, for example, and they have a big impact on anyone working under them. But those workers are less than 3% of the total workforce. Similarly, our military is a key element of our international relations, yet there's only one military personnel for every 2.75 civil servants.

The other interesting element is how these numbers change over time. The military was almost three times larger 50 years ago than today. And considering we had a smaller population, a much larger proportion of people were in the armed forces back then. On the up: the self-employed. This group has doubled over a similar period, increasing the UK's entrepreneurial presence with them.

All figures rounded to the nearest thousand, unless otherwise stated.

## 17%
Proportion of employees who work more than 45 hours a week (2018)

## 25%
Proportion of self-employed people who work more than 45 hours a week (2018)

## 2.5m
Number of people who want to work more than they currently do (2017)
Either want an additional job, want more hours in current job or want a job with more hours.

**TOTAL NUMBER OF WORKERS (2017)**

By headcount and based on December 2017 figures.

## 32,24

## 1,639,000
Total NHS staff (2017)
By headcount and based on December 2017 figures.

## 427,000
Civil servants (2017)
By headcount and based on December 2017 figures.
Excludes Northern Ireland's civil service.

## 155,000
HM Forces (2017)
By headcount and based on December 2017 figures.

# 1 in 9

People work flexi-time (2017)

# 1 in 264

People job-share (2017)

# 901,000

Number of zero-hour contracts (2017)
Based on October to December figures.

# 1.1m

Number of people with a second job (2018)

# 8,000

# 4,840,000

Number of self-employed people
Based on figures for October to December 2018.

# 100%

Approximate growth of
self-employed people from
December 1964 to December 2014

# COMPANIES IN THE UK

Services dominate the UK economy. They represent about 80% of private sector employees and companies in the UK, and about the same proportion of our economic output. Manufacturing has far fewer companies and employs less than a tenth of those working in services, while construction employs even fewer people but has more than double the number of companies compared with manufacturing.

What are we to make of all this? Well sectors are not made equal. Some require big companies that can operate at scale.

This is evident in the mining and quarrying sector, which is made up primarily of oil and gas companies. There are fewer of them but they tend to employ more people. On the other end of the scale, agricultural companies tend to be small, employing three people on average and providing just 1% of all jobs. Everything else falls somewhere in the middle, depending on the structure of the market and the product or service. Yet, understanding these differences and what drives each of these companies can lead us to better policies for employment and growth.

See Notes for additional details on industry categorisation. Data from 2017.

TOP 10 INDUSTRIES BY NUMBER OF COMPANIES

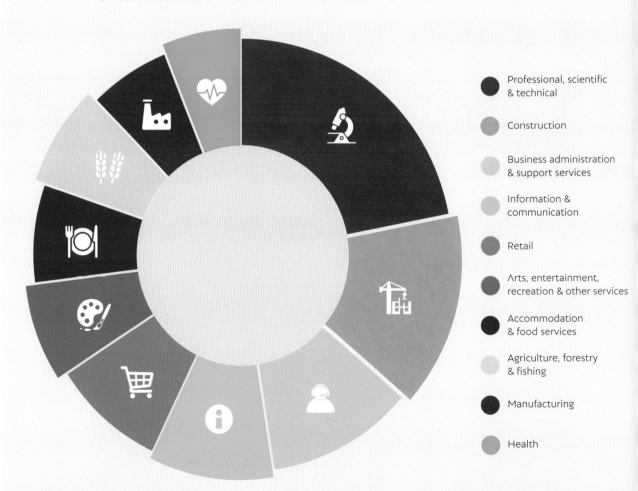

- Professional, scientific & technical
- Construction
- Business administration & support services
- Information & communication
- Retail
- Arts, entertainment, recreation & other services
- Accommodation & food services
- Agriculture, forestry & fishing
- Manufacturing
- Health

# TOP 5 INDUSTRIES BY COUNTRY & NUMBER OF COMPANIES

# COMPANY SIZE BY EMPLOYEE NUMBERS

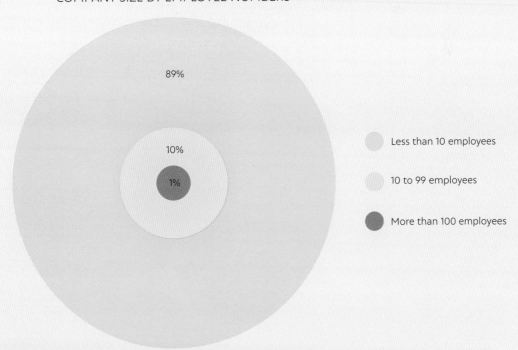

89%

10%

1%

Less than 10 employees

10 to 99 employees

More than 100 employees

# COMPANIES AND INDUSTRIES BY REGION

Often, businesses are located where they are for historical reasons – the founders may have lived there at the time they were founded. Still, business locations can change for a variety of reasons. What's interesting is the shift in business activities across the country and across industries. Who would have thought that Winchester has more companies per 1,000 people than London, Cardiff, Edinburgh or Glasgow? The entrepreneurial spirit knows no borders.

When comparing registered companies over time and across the country, it's obvious that the number of manufacturing companies has decreased in the past 20 years or so. But the number of financial companies has also shrunk since 2010. Yet the number of companies overall has increased significantly since 1998.

On an industry basis, agriculture has barely moved and production companies (which includes mining activities as well as utilities and manufacturing) have decreased by about 8,000 firms. On the up side, construction has grown by almost 170,000 companies, but it's service-based firms that have led the charge and boosted the number of business by 70% over the 20 years in question.

Industry classifications changed in 2007 so industry-based figures either side of this year are based on different classifications. Data from 2018 unless otherwise specified.

**506,180**
Number of companies
registered in London

**157,095**
Number of UK manufacturing
businesses in 1998

**2,669,440**
Number of UK businesses in 2018

**136,120**
Number of UK manufacturing
businesses in 2018

**60%**
Proportion of companies
with more than
£100k in sales

**-6,530**
Change in the number
of financial companies
from 2010 to 2018

**34,565**
Number of companies
registered in Birmingham

**19%**
Proportion of UK
businesses registered
in London

# CITY BUSINESSES PER 1,000 PEOPLE

Aberdeen **38**

Stirling **41**

Glasgow **30**

Edinburgh **36**

Newcastle upon Tyne **27**

Carlisle **44**

Sunderland **20**

Belfast **29**

Lancaster **32**

Leeds **36**

York **34**

Kingston upon Hull **23**

Liverpool **30**

Manchester **44**

Lichfield **51**

Nottingham **27**

Norwich **33**

Birmingham **30**

Cambridge **40**

Worcester **30**

St Albans **61**

Gloucester **28**

Chelmsford **45**

Swansea **26**

Bristol **39**

London **57**

Cardiff **31**

Canterbury **32**

Winchester **63**

Exeter **32**

Brighton and Hove **48**

Plymouth **22**

Company data represent a snapshot of March 2018 whereas population estimates are 2017 mid-year estimates.

# THE GREAT BRITISH COMMUTE

We sometimes project our own experiences onto others. When working in London it's hard to imagine anyone driving to work. How would you ever park? I now work in South Wales and some are surprised I commute by train. Almost three-quarters of us head to work on four wheels and 90% of those go by car or van. Roughly half of drivers are women, while men are far more likely to be the ones on motorbikes or bicycles. Six out of 10 walkers are women, which might go part way to explaining why the longest commutes

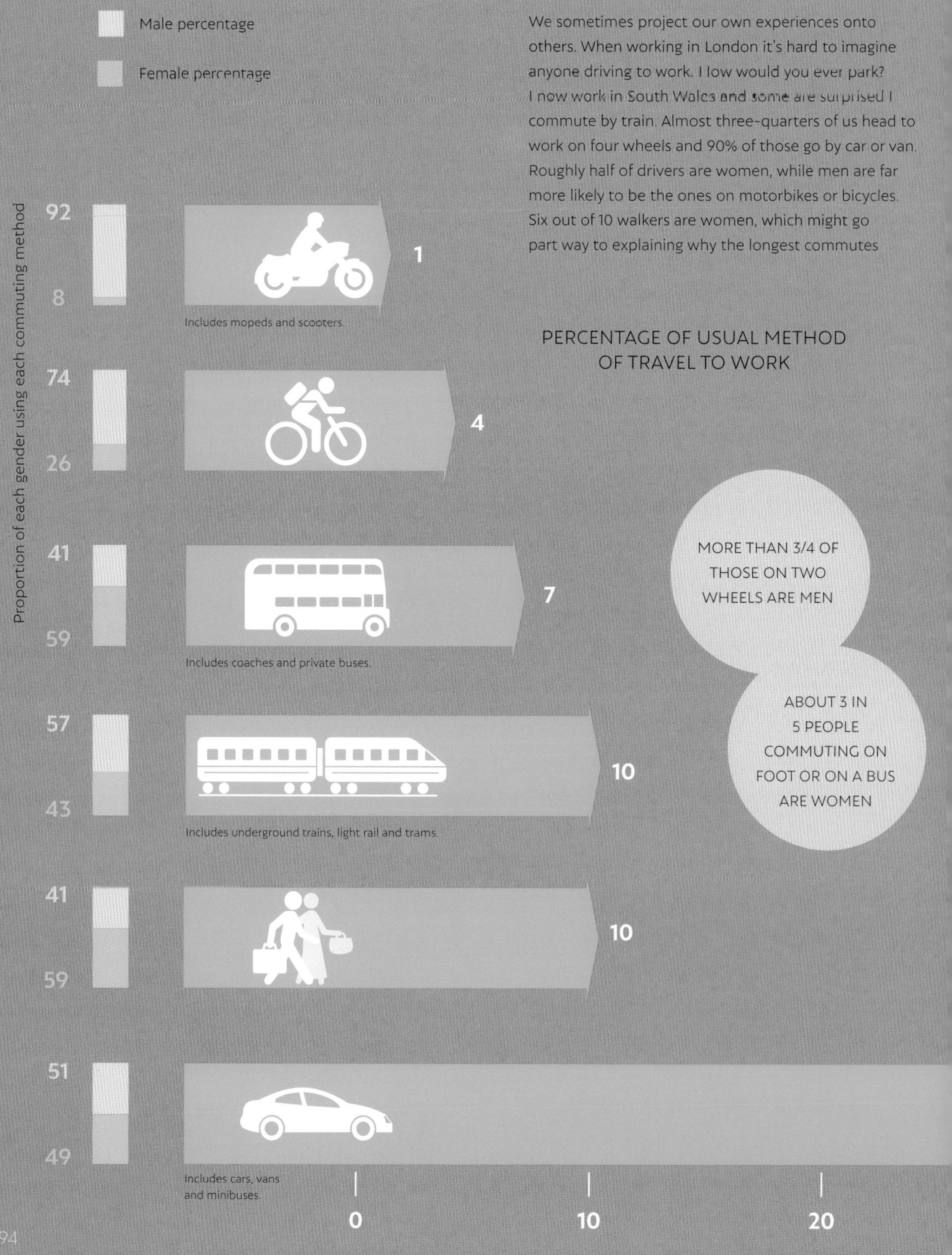

## PERCENTAGE OF USUAL METHOD OF TRAVEL TO WORK

Male percentage

Female percentage

Proportion of each gender using each commuting method

92
8
**1**
Includes mopeds and scooters.

74
26
**4**

41
59
**7**
Includes coaches and private buses.

57
43
**10**
Includes underground trains, light rail and trams.

41
59
**10**

51
49
Includes cars, vans and minibuses.

0    10    20

MORE THAN 3/4 OF THOSE ON TWO WHEELS ARE MEN

ABOUT 3 IN 5 PEOPLE COMMUTING ON FOOT OR ON A BUS ARE WOMEN

are done by men. These are self-reported numbers, so while peoples' main method of commuting should be easy for them to determine, the length taken is easy to misestimate. It's unclear whether people would under or over-estimate their commute or whether this would differ between genders, so there's a chance the inaccuracies balance out. Either way, you should feel lucky you're not part of the 6% or so of Brits who commute for more than an hour. Or most of you should.

Data from 2017.

## TIME TAKEN TO TRAVEL TO WORK (MINUTES)

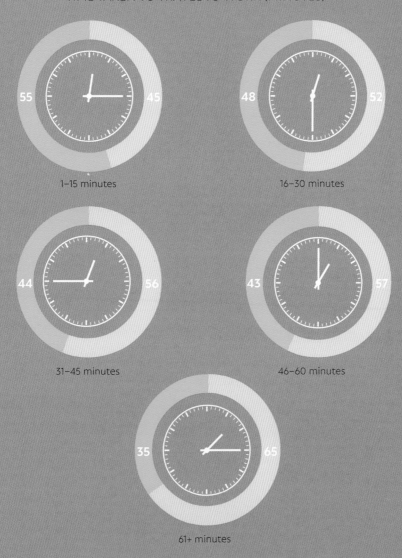

# EMPLOYMENT TRENDS

Employment is a funny thing: we all think we know what the figures mean, but many people are unaware of how the numbers are put together. Unemployment figures come from a survey. If people don't have a job then they're asked if they're looking for work. Only those that say yes are unemployed, the rest are categorised as inactive. The unemployment rate (shown in the graph below) excludes those who are inactive (retirees, students, carers etc).

Yet figures for inactive people (those not looking for work) provide interesting insights. The number of

inactive Pakistani and Bangladeshi women is above 50%. To be sure, these are small populations of people in the UK and surveying small populations increases the risk of sampling error, but even accounting for sampling error, these numbers are high. It's also notable that for every ethnicity, women are more likely to be inactive than men, whereas the unemployment rates are about the same. Part of this effect is down to retired women living longer, but women are still more likely to take child-care related breaks from work, which would explain an important element of the gap.

## UNEMPLOYMENT RATES OCT–DEC 2018, UK

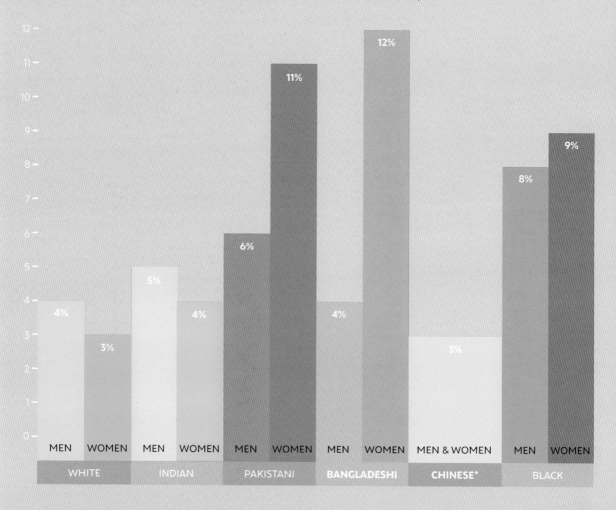

* Data for unemployment by gender for those of Chinese ethnicity are unreliable due to small sample sizes, so the average for both genders combined is displayed instead.

# EMPLOYMENT STATUS BY ETHNICITY & GENDER FOR PEOPLE AGED 16–64, Oct–Dec 2018

## MEN

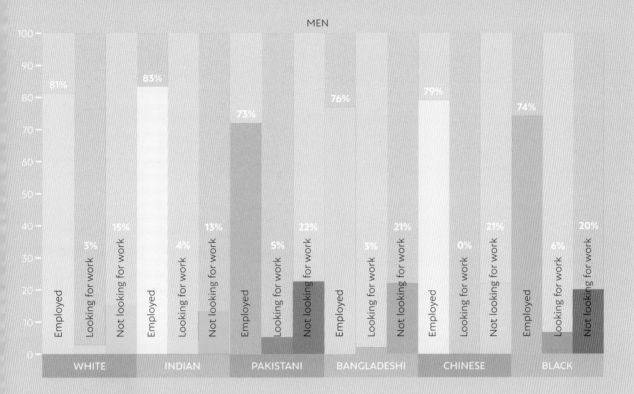

## WOMEN

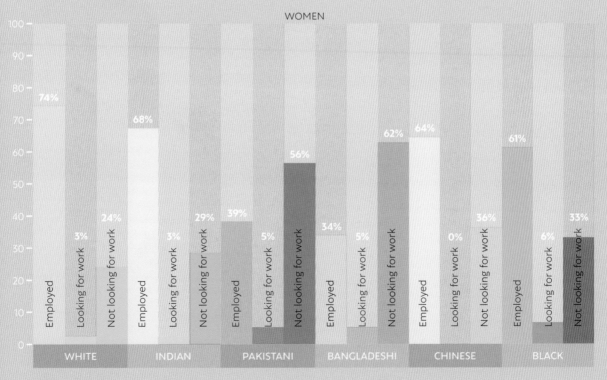

Proportions may not sum to 100% due to rounding.

# SELF–EMPLOYMENT

More women of all ethnicities have been taking up self-employment. The rise is not limited to women, but women have been driving a shift to higher self-employment rates over the past 15 years.

Despite these rises, the proportion of Chinese people taking up self-employment has fallen from 2002 levels. To be clear, the number of self-employed Chinese people has increased, but at a slower rate than the number of Chinese people in the UK. In contrast, the number of Bangladeshi entrepreneurs has increased significantly since 2002. The increase is largest for men, at around 30,000 additional business owners over the period, but the rise for women is equally notable. That's because in 2002 less than 1% were entrepreneurs – the lowest of any ethnicity in the UK. Some 15 years and more than 4.5 million female self-starters later and 3% of Bangladeshi women are now self-employed. That's still lower than women from other ethnic groups, but it's also the largest growth rate of any ethnicity.

Although there's an important element to consider with statistics like this: Chinese people made up just 0.5% of the workforce in 2017 (less than 160,000 people). Bangladeshi women are just 0.2% (less than 60,000). With survey samples of such small numbers of people, the results can vary quite widely. Long-term trends can still hold and the recent self-employed uptick is clear for Bangladeshi men and women. With Chinese entrepreneurs, the trend is more mixed, with an average of 15% being self-employed over the past 15 years. That might be a closer estimate than either that of 2002 or 2017.

Data from 2017.

## PERCENTAGE MAKE-UP OF EMPLOYED

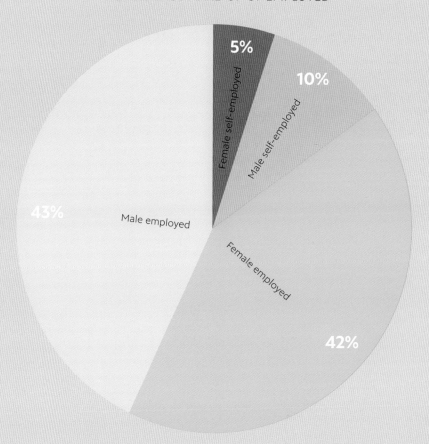

- 5% Female self-employed
- 10% Male self-employed
- 43% Male employed
- 42% Female employed

# RATIO OF SELF-EMPLOYED TO EMPLOYED

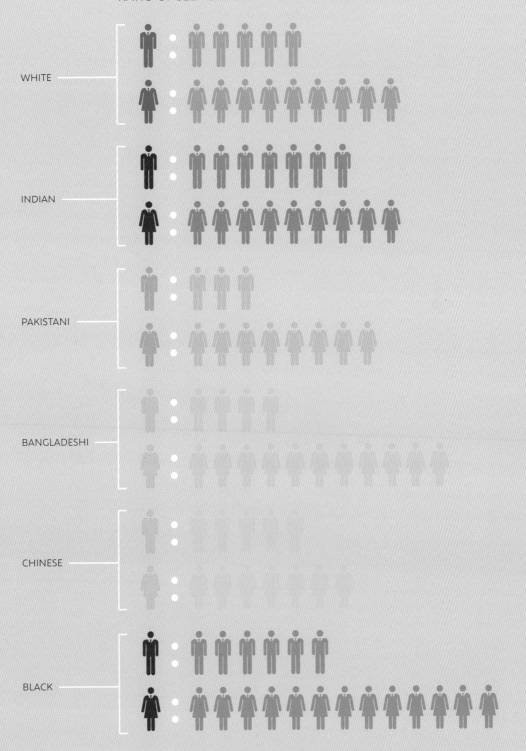

The more people on the right, the less likely that group is to be self-employed.

# IMMIGRATION BY OCCUPATION

Most Brits know that the rate of immigration increased more rapidly in the 2000s than during the previous decade. Go beyond the figures for net immigration and most of us are making educated guesses based, in part, on what we've heard or read and our own experiences. Some are more informed than others, but rarely do we delve into more detail.

These data come from surveys at UK ports of entry. They ask those moving countries what they were doing before they moved and I've focused on non-Brits to give an indication of the kinds of people who move to and from Britain.

By splitting immigration inflows from outflows, it's possible to see that in almost every situation, the number of people moving increased, just by different rates. The only exception is the number of children leaving the UK which fell by more than 40,000 kids from one decade to the next.

For all categories, the growth rate for those coming to the UK increased from the 1990s to the noughties more than the growth rate for those leaving the UK did in the same period. This is most notable for students, where there were five people arriving in the 2000s for every two in the 1990s. And whereas half as many students left in the 1990s as came in, this dropped to a third in the noughties.

Yet the biggest change in terms of growth was for those who were doing manual or clerical work before arriving. There were more than three times as many who moved to the UK in the 2000s as there were over the previous decade. Those leaving more than doubled, but the net effect was that four and a half times as many people with manual and clerical experience came to the UK in the noughties as did in the 1990s. To be clear, there were less manual and clerical workers coming to the UK than managers, professionals and students in both periods. The number of people leaving is comparable for all three. Yet sometimes the rate of change that people see is what's important. Other times it's the actual numbers that count. And sometimes it's both.

Unfortunately, we don't know what these people did when they entered the UK as we don't use this survey to follow their lives once they've moved. We're left to guess, although you hopefully now feel better informed to do so.

93

403

77

517

204

273

120

513

278

79

Professional
& managerial

Manual
& clerical

Students

Other
adults

Children

222

903

1,200

235

1,208

289

515

474

186

151

Outflows (thousands)

2000s   1990s

Inflows (thousands)

2000s   1990s

101

# WHY IMMIGRANTS COME TO THE UK

Three out of every five EU citizens who moved to the UK in the noughties did so for work. For non-EU citizens this drops to 1 in 3, with almost 40% of them coming instead to study. For those who did come for work, about three-quarters already had a job, no matter if they were from the EU or not.

However, as soon as you dip into more granular data, there's much greater variety in the reasons for coming to the UK.

Half of non-EU Europeans moved for work and of those, 9 out of 10 had a job before arriving. Another 3 out of 10 came to study. Compare that with Asians where half of them were heading to classes, 1 in 5 had secured a job and 1 in 4 were accompanying someone. We can go even further into the differences and look at different parts of Asia to find that 75% of people from East Asia

NORTH AMERICA

CENTRAL AND
SOUTH AMERICA

| Have a job | Looking for work | Accompanying someone | Studying | Other |
|---|---|---|---|---|
| 486,000 | 176,000 | 79,000 | 249,000 | 99,000 |
| 59,000 | 6,000 | 23,000 | 40,000 | 7,000 |
| 286,000 | 45,000 | 366,000 | 731,000 | 63,000 |
| 96,000 | 54,000 | 105,000 | 128,000 | 67,000 |
| 67,000 | 17,000 | 59,000 | 85,000 | 71,000 |
| 17,000 | 6,000 | 17,000 | 38,000 | 3,000 |
| 75,000 | 93,000 | 26,000 | 6,000 | 109,000 |

(mostly China, Korea and Japan) came to study compared with 40% for South and South East Asia.

From a high level, it's easy to make assumptions about why people would leave one country or region to go to another. But situations do differ and it's interesting to note how these differences manifest themselves across the globe. And international relations, visa rules and distances do matter. After all, barely any Aussies come this far to study, but plenty come looking for a job. Working holiday visas, perhaps?

See Notes for details on categories used in this image. Data from 2000 to 2009 and rounded to the nearst thousand.

# PROFESSION BY GENDER

We have been through several waves of feminism, yet certain quarters of the labour market have been slow to address gender inequality. Women are still over-represented in administrative and secretarial roles; they are far more likely than men to work in caring professions and leisure services. Similarly, men are far more likely to be in a skilled trade than women. They are also more likely to work in a plant or factory setting.

Yet some areas are changing. Men are still more likely to be managers, but the difference has narrowed to five percentage points (13% of men hold these positions versus 8% of women). And women are more likely than men to work in a profession. We're not at parity yet, but these occupations are leading the charge towards equality. The others may be due for a shake-up.

Data from 2017.

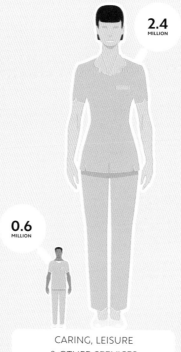

**2.4** MILLION

**0.6** MILLION

CARING, LEISURE & OTHER SERVICES

**2.5** MILLION

**0.8** MILLION

ADMINISTRATIVE & SECRETARIAL

**2.6** MILLION

**2** MILLION

ASSOCIATE PROFESSIONAL & TECHNICAL

**1.8** MILLION

**0.2** MILLION

PROCESS, PLANT & MACHINE OPERATIVES

PROFESSIONAL OCCUPATIONS

MANAGERS, DIRECTORS &
SENIOR OFFICIALS

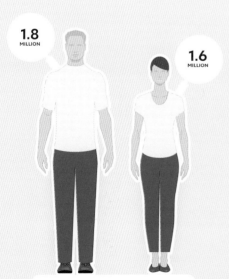

ELEMENTARY
OCCUPATIONS

SKILLED TRADES

SALES &
CUSTOMER SERVICES

# ETHNICITIES BY PROFESSION

Is there any reason why a person from an ethnic minority shouldn't become a manager? Clearly not. Almost 6% of black people hold a managerial or director-level job. Yet that's half the proportion of white people who reach the same position. Of course, there could be cultural differences. That might explain why almost a third of those with Indian heritage are professionals, notably higher than the average 20% of workers. And maybe education plays a role – few would argue that education quality is evenly distributed and black kids might be missing out on the best opportunities. But let's be honest: at the very least black people face unfavourable unconscious bias and in many cases this is, in fact, outright discrimination.

This is nothing new. But facing these issues (and using data to demonstrate the situation) is a necessary step to fixing them.

Data from 2017.
* Mixed ethnic group data represent those family backgrounds that fall into more than one ethnic group. Due to small samples, it is not possible to disaggregate black, African, Caribbean and black British into seperate groups. Numbers may not sum up to 100% due to rounding.

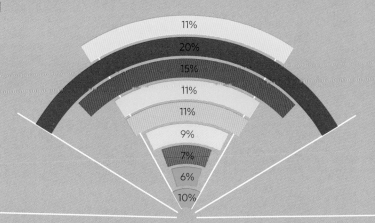

WHITE

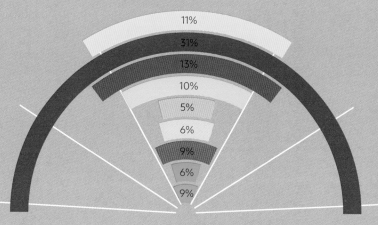

INDIAN

- Managers
- Professionals
- Technical & associate professionals
- Administrative & secretarial occupations
- Skilled trades
- Caring, leisure & other occupations
- Sales & customer service
- Plant & machine operatives
- Elementary occupations

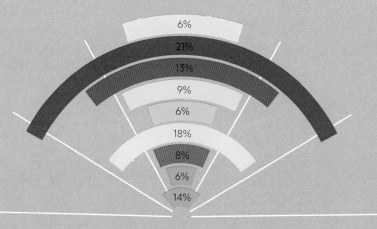

BLACK OR BLACK BRITISH

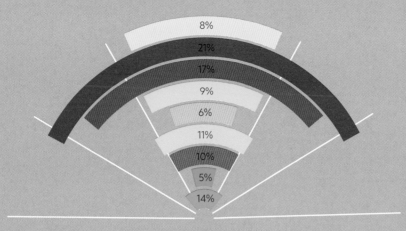

8%
21%
17%
9%
6%
11%
10%
5%
14%

MIXED ETHNIC GROUPS*

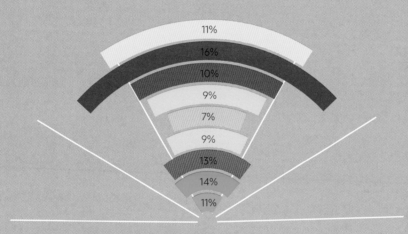

11%
16%
10%
9%
7%
9%
13%
14%
11%

PAKISTANI/BANGLADESHI

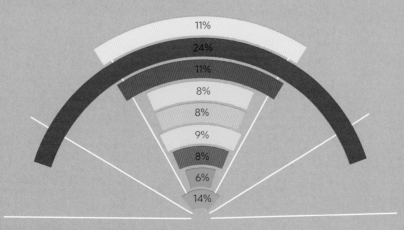

11%
24%
11%
8%
8%
9%
8%
6%
14%

OTHER ETHNIC GROUPS

## AVERAGE WEEKLY HOURS BY INDUSTRY, 2017

| Industry | January to March | April to June |
|---|---|---|
| AGRICULTURE, FORESTRY & FISHING | 44 | 44 |
| MINING, ENERGY & WATER SUPPLY | 38 | 38 |
| CONSTRUCTION | 38 | 38 |
| MANUFACTURING | 37 | 37 |
| IT & MEDIA | 37 | 37 |
| TRANSPORT & STORAGE | 36 | 35 |
| FINANCE, INSURANCE & REAL ESTATE | 35 | 34 |
| PROFESSIONAL & TECHNICAL | 35 | 34 |
| PUBLIC SERVICES | 33 | 33 |
| ADMINISTRATION | 31 | 31 |
| RETAIL & CAR TRADES | 31 | 30 |
| HEALTH & SOCIAL WORK | 30 | 29 |
| ACCOMMODATION & FOOD SERVICES | 28 | 28 |
| EDUCATION | 30 | 28 |

## WORKING HOURS

How many hours did you work last week? Some people will find this question easier to answer than others, although few are likely to nail the exact amount. You might even overestimate: no one wants to be seen as lazy.

But do these inaccuracies matter? Well it depends on what you're measuring. If you want to know how hours have changed or how different industries compare, then the data might be good enough – assuming you ask enough people and they're all off (or overestimating) by about the same degree. These are assumptions, but we require such assumptions in statistics because we lack perfect knowledge.

With the knowledge we do have, we can tell that farmers, on average, work far longer hours than anyone else. No surprise for farmers. But the difference is stark: depending on the time of year, they work between five and nine hours a week more than any other industry. Add this up over a year and these differences are significant.

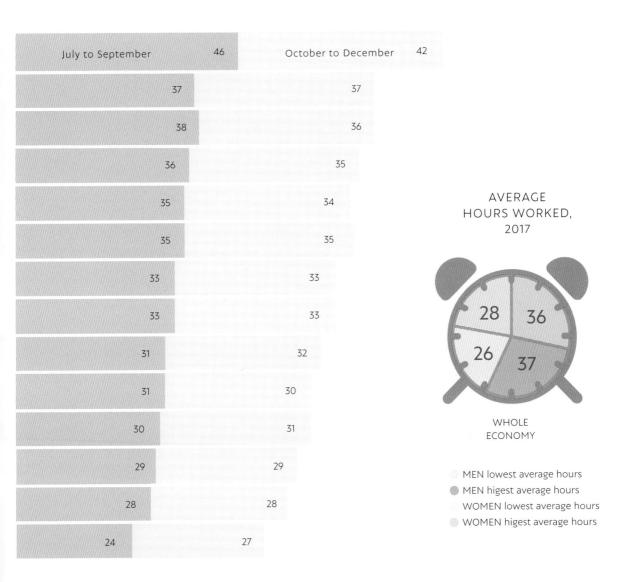

| July to September | 46 | October to December | 42 |
|---|---|---|---|
| | 37 | | 37 |
| | 38 | | 36 |
| | 36 | | 35 |
| | 35 | | 34 |
| | 35 | | 35 |
| | 33 | | 33 |
| | 33 | | 33 |
| | 31 | | 32 |
| | 31 | | 30 |
| | 30 | | 31 |
| | 29 | | 29 |
| | 28 | | 28 |
| | 24 | | 27 |

AVERAGE
HOURS WORKED,
2017

28  36
26  37

WHOLE
ECONOMY

○ MEN lowest average hours
● MEN higest average hours
  WOMEN lowest average hours
⦿ WOMEN higest average hours

If our farmers want a shorter working week, then they could consider teaching, although this comes with the widest variation of hours across the year. If they're looking for stable hours, then maybe the hospitality industry is better.

Does gender matter for hours worked? On the face of it, there's no reason why women and men should work different hours. Women do tend to work part time more often, yet there's still a difference between full-time hours for women and men. Or maybe men overestimate their hours more. And, of course, these are paid hours so they ignore any unpaid work such as caring for people (children or the elderly) and housework.

If self-reported hours are too inaccurate for you, then you could always ask employers – they should know how many hours their employees work. The trouble is employers tend to report contracted hours and they rarely log unpaid overtime. Surveying employers also excludes a particularly hard-working bunch of people: the self-employed.

See Notes for further details on industries.

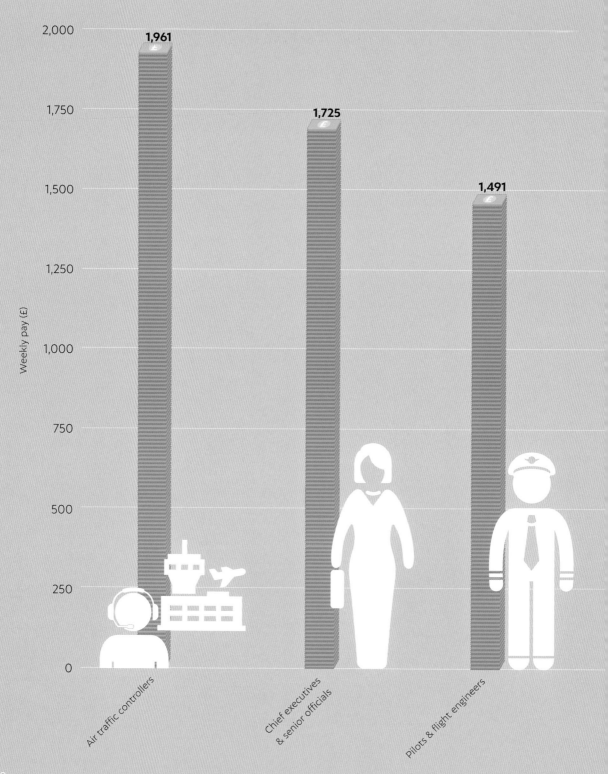

HIGHEST AND LOWEST PAID PROFESSIONS, 2018

Weekly pay (£)

2,000 — **1,961**

1,750 — **1,725**

1,500 — **1,491**

1,250

1,000

750

500

250

0

Air traffic controllers

Chief executives & senior officials

Pilots & flight engineers

# JOBS THAT PAY WELL... AND THOSE THAT DON'T

During a particularly tough week at work I looked at our receptionist and thought, 'He must have a low-stress job. Why don't I do that?' But when looking at the list of high-paid professions it seems that stress and/or responsibility for a large number of lives align with large salaries. That's not to say that florists – or receptionists – have stress-free lives. Based on these data, they're likely to stress about their finances for a start.

However, there are some things to consider with these data. The sample represents about 1% of the population selected via National Insurance numbers and only employees are selected (so no florist owners in these data). It's a stable survey, so it provides a consistent timeseries of data (i.e. the same people) and it's an excellent source for hours and wages by a host of categories – a lot of gender pay-gap data come from this survey, for example. Despite the great coverage, sampling small populations (such as pilots) results in less reliability.

The results for air traffic controllers, pilots, florists and lollipop ladies are all considered 'acceptable', while the other estimates are 'precise'. So if you want to be sure of a high wage, chief exec is the job for you. But air traffic controller is also a good bet. Then again, money isn't everything. Maybe I'll apply for that receptionist role next week.

Data relate to full-time employees on adult rate whose pay for the survey period was unaffected by absence. 'Full-time' is defined as employees working more than 30 paid hours per week (or 25 or more for the teaching professions).

307 Hairdressers & barbers

301 Lollipop ladies

288 Florists

# THE GENDER PAY GAP

When we think about our own wage, we might refer to our annual pay packet. Or what enters our bank each month. Or maybe what we get paid on an hourly basis. These are different things, but each gives us a measure of comparison.

And so it is with the gender pay gap: there's no such thing as one pay gap. The gap will differ if considered on an hourly rate or on an annual salary basis. The data here represent gross annual pay, which will include performance pay (bonuses or commissions) as well as a basic. That might make it less accurate as a measure of the pay gap, but at the most fundamental level we're most interested in what people actually earn and how that differs between men and women.

Furthermore, the gap will vary over time. It starts relatively low when youngsters enter the workforce, then grows at quite a rate before subsiding slightly as people approach retirement. This reflects our culture around women taking time out of work when they have kids, sometimes returning on a part-time basis. It possibly reflects men being more brazen when asking for a rise.

Yet there's more to it than that. When considered on an hourly basis, the gap tends to narrow as men tend to work more paid hours than women. And the hourly rate provides insights (and potentially a good signpost for young women entering the workforce) into which industries have the best and worst performance on this measure.

Unfortunately, the signpost, for the most part, points to lower-paid professions where the gap tends to be narrower (and occasionally in women's favour). Yet there is a glimmer of hope: the gap is notable but relatively low for professionals. This helps those with good degrees but that does leave women without qualifications in even lower-paid positions than their peers (whether those peers are other women or the men they work with).

Data from 2017.

MALE

FEMALE

## MEDIAN WAGE (£)

Managers, directors & senior officials
44,500
33,600

Professional occupations
40,700
31,000

Associate professional & technical occupations
34,200
25,900

Administrative & secretarial occupations
23,400
17,300

Skilled trade occupations
27,200
15,800

Caring, leisure & other service occupations
18,200
13,400

Sales & customer service occupations
17,300
11,400

Process, plant & machine operatives
24,700
16,900

Elementary occupations
18,700
8,400

Rounded to the nearest hundred.

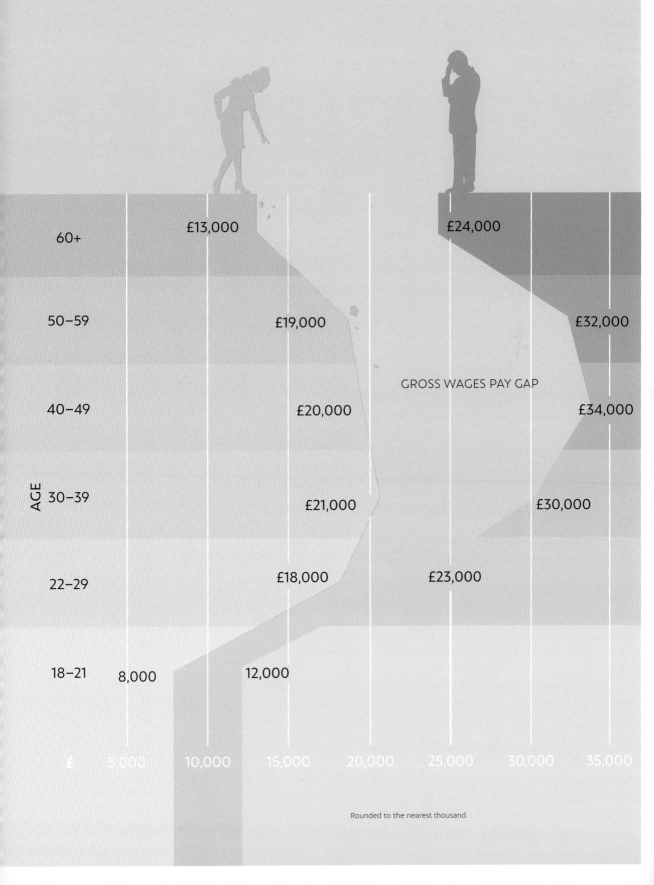

£13,000

£24,000

60+

50–59

£19,000

£32,000

40–49

£20,000

GROSS WAGES PAY GAP

£34,000

AGE

30–39

£21,000

£30,000

22–29

£18,000

£23,000

18–21        8,000        12,000

£        5,000        10,000        15,000        20,000        25,000        30,000        35,000

Rounded to the nearest thousand.

# LABOUR DISPUTES

If you're asked to name a time when strikes had a large effect on British life, chances are you might think of the Winter of Discontent in 1979 or the miners' strikes of the 1970s and 80s. These are within living memory, but in terms of the number of working days lost (the days where work stopped multiplied by the number of people striking), the strikes of the 1920s had a much larger effect.

Of these, the General Strike of 1926 towers over all others. That's largely because, when the miners downed tools over pay and conditions, other industries joined the cause in solidarity. The following year, sympathy strikes were made illegal.

Although the number of working days lost through strikes in the 1970s was less than half that of the 1920s, the 70s saw record numbers of work stoppages. The number of strikes grew through the 1950s, somewhat stabilised (around the new, higher level) in the 1960s and reached a peak in 1970 when workers downed tools more than 3,900 times.

The occurrence of strikes remained high in the 1970s but reduced dramatically from 1980 and it has been relatively subdued ever since. This is due to many things, not least changes to laws around strikes. It's also far easier for trade unions to organise labour when there are large employers whose employees work in close proximity – like in factories and coal mines – and there's a lot less of this kind of work around now.

Excludes strikes involving less than 10 workers or lasting less than a day (unless working days lost is 100 days or more).

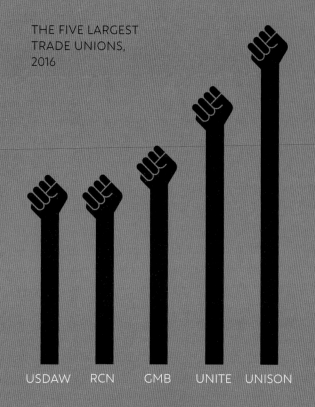

## THE FIVE LARGEST TRADE UNIONS, 2016

USDAW    RCN    GMB    UNITE    UNISON

USDAW: Union of Shop, Distributive and Allied Workers
RCN: Royal College of Nursing
GMB: General, Municipal, Boilermakers and Allied Trade Union

Trade union membership figures are for UK residents only and exclude trade union federations, such as the Trade Union Congress (TUC). In 2017, the National Union of Teachers merged with the Association of Teachers and Lecturers. At the time of writing, they have yet to publish an annual return.

## NOTABLE STRIKES
Total number of working days lost in year

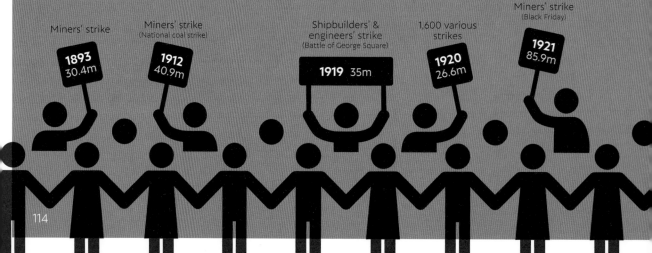

Miners' strike
**1893** 30.4m

Miners' strike
(National coal strike)
**1912** 40.9m

Shipbuilders' & engineers' strike
(Battle of George Square)
**1919** 35m

1,600 various strikes
**1920** 26.6m

Miners' strike
(Black Friday)
**1921** 85.9m

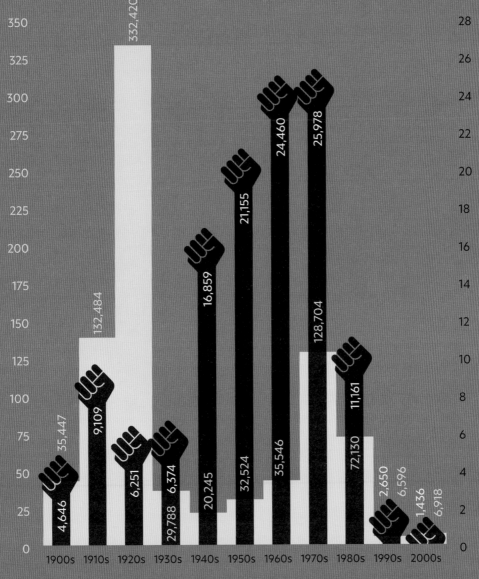

| | | | | | | | | | | | |
|---|---|---|---|---|---|---|---|---|---|---|---|
| 350 | | | 332,420 | | | | | | | | 28 |
| 325 | | | | | | | | | | | 26 |
| 300 | | | | | | 24,460 | 25,978 | | | | 24 |
| 275 | | | | | | | | | | | 22 |
| 250 | | | | 21,155 | | | | | | | 20 |
| 225 | | | | | | | | | | | 18 |
| 200 | | | | 16,859 | | | | | | | 16 |
| 175 | | | | | | | | | | | 14 |
| 150 | 132,484 | | | | | | 128,704 | | | | 12 |
| 125 | | | | | | | | | | | 10 |
| 100 | 9,109 | | | | | | 11,161 | | | | 8 |
| 75 | | 6,251 | 6,374 | | | 35,546 | 72,130 | | | | 6 |
| 50 | 35,447 | | | 20,245 | 32,524 | | | | | | 4 |
| 25 | 4,646 | | 29,788 | | | | | 2,650 | 6,596 | 1,436 / 6,918 | 2 |
| 0 | | | | | | | | | | | 0 |

1900s  1910s  1920s  1930s  1940s  1950s  1960s  1970s  1980s  1990s  2000s

□ Working days lost due to strikes (thousands)
✊ Number of strikes (thousands)

**600 various strikes**
**1922**
19.9m

**General Strike**
(Unions joined striking miners)
**1926** 162.2m

**Miners' strike**
(UK miners' strike)
**1972**
23.9m

**Public sector strikes**
(Winter of Discontent)
**1979** 29.5m

**Miners' strike**
(Battle of Orgreave)
**1984**
27.1m

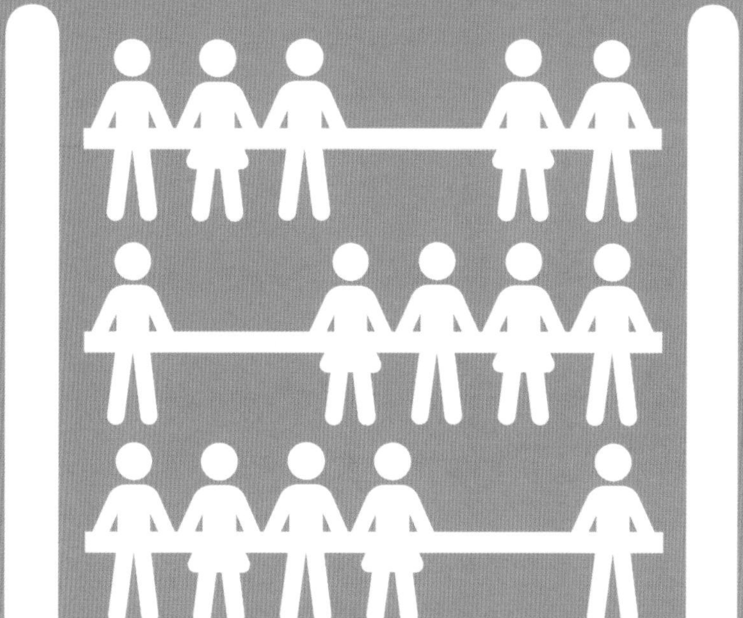

# PERSONAL FINANCE

# HOUSEHOLD SPENDING

Averages for spending data are fascinating: we spent more on recreation in 2016 than we did on housing costs. Our spending on restaurants and hotels was almost double our spending on clothes and footwear.

What's more, data like these provide insights into how we change our spending: food bills have gone from 16% of our total spend in 2000/01 to 10% in 2016/17. We're also spending a smaller proportion of our money on alcohol and tobacco. These comparisons can be difficult to make as spending categories change over time to keep up with modern life. And surveys change as well. These lead to better estimates, but they also make it more difficult to compare data over time.

The other thing to be aware of are the issues with using averages, which are useful for overall trends, but mask important differences. For example, those on lower incomes probably spend a higher proportion of their earnings on the basics (food, shelter, transport etc). And spending differs with age, family situation, location... The data that are most important to consider will depend on the question you're trying to answer.

Averages can also look strange. In the following pages you will see a rent payments figure of less than £2,000 a year and secondary education fees of £57 a year. For many households these figures will be zero. For others, they will be much more significant. But for the average, they're £2,000 and £57 a year.

Then there are the data quirks: does laundry and dry cleaning fall into clothing, household services, miscellaneous or something else? Choose a category from this page and check out the sources in the Notes to see if the international classification agrees with you.

Figures represent total annual household expenditure (£ millions), 2016/17.
* Housing costs represent a net figure and exclude mortgage interest payments, council tax and Northern Ireland rates. Rent payments included in housing costs exclude housing benefit and any housing rebates or allowances received.

TRANSPORT £113,175

RECREATION & CULTURE £104,357

HOUSING COSTS* £103,001

OTHER EXPENDITURE ITEMS £102,218

FOOD &
NON-ALCOHOLIC
DRINKS
£82,338

MISCELLANEOUS
GOODS & SERVICES
£59,275

HOUSEHOLD GOODS
& SERVICES
£55,831

ALCOHOL, TOBACCO
& NARCOTICS
£16,958

RESTAURANTS & HOTELS
£71,067

CLOTHING &
FOOTWEAR
£35,690

COMMUNICATION
£24,367

HEALTH COSTS
£10,436

EDUCATION
£8,140

# THE GREAT BRITISH MEAL

If we spend about four times as much on chocolate as we do on tea, does that mean we like chocolate about four times more than tea? What's missing here is the quantity of tea we're buying at these figures, but if the above did hold then we'd truly be in love with meat. It's the item that takes up more cash in our weekly shop than any other.

It could be that meat is more expensive, pound for pound, than other items. If we halved our spending on beef, pork and the rest, then we could quadruple the amount of beer and cider we buy. Although that may not be the best idea. Increasing restaurant meals by a third is a more inviting option.

Figures represent average annual household expenditure, 2016/17.

RESTAURANT
& CAFÉ MEALS
£441

TEA
£26

FISH & SEAFOOD
£141

FRESH FRUIT
£198

FRESH VEGETABLES
£214

MEAT
£647

CHOCOLATE
£99

BUNS, CAKES
& BISCUITS
£193
Includes crispbread & puddings.

TAKEAWAY MEALS
(eaten at home)
£266

OTHER TAKEAWAY
& SNACK FOOD
£261

COFFEE
£47

WORKPLACE
MEALS
£52

SOFT DRINKS
£94

SCHOOL MEALS
£37

WINES
(brought home)
£214

BEER, LAGER & CIDER
(brought home)
£115

SPIRITS
(brought home)
£94
Includes liqueurs.

# LOOKING GREAT, BRITAIN

At first glance, the stereotype of women owning lots of shoes doesn't hold up in the data. Women do spend about £1.25 on shoes for every £1 spent by men, although this hardly seems like a closet-full versus a few pairs. If the stereotype is representative, then there must either be quite a price disparity between men and women's shoes or women keep their shoes for longer.

The bigger disparity between the sexes seems to be the amount spent on clothes, where women spend 70% more than men. Nearly half of all spending

## FOOTWEAR

- WOMEN'S FOOTWEAR
  £125

- MEN'S FOOTWEAR
  £99

- KIDS' FOOTWEAR
  £42

## CLOTHING

- WOMEN'S CLOTHING
  £522

- MEN'S CLOTHING
  £303

- KIDS' CLOTHING
  £157

- CLOTHING ACCESSORIES
  £37

on clothes goes on women's apparel, with kids' clothes making up the rest. There are no gender splits for accessories or hair and beauty products, so I'll leave you to determine where this lies.

Figures represent average annual household expenditure, 2016/17.

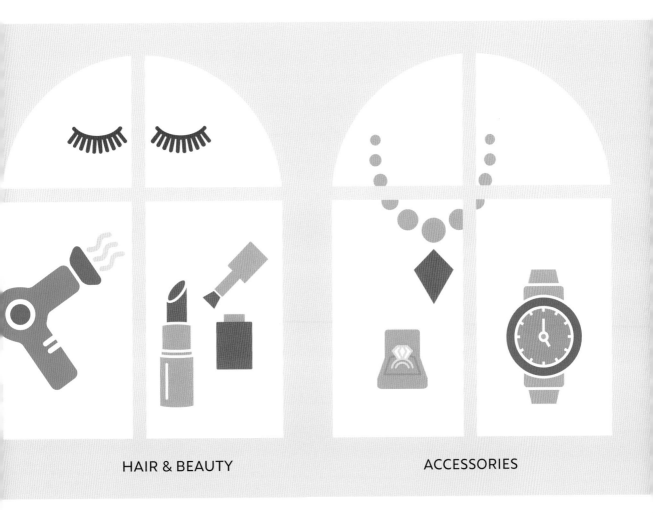

## HAIR & BEAUTY

## ACCESSORIES

HAIR & BEAUTY TREATMENTS
£219

HAIR PRODUCTS
£47

COSMETICS & RELATED ACCESSORIES
£172

WATCHES, JEWELLERY & PERSONAL EFFECTS
£110

# THE GREAT BRITISH NIGHT OUT

Ever noticed how many pubs and bars there are in the UK?
We love a night out in our local and these little visits add up
to quite a bit over time – drinks in bars and pubs dominate
our spending in the area for every age group.

Figures represent average annual household expenditure, 2016/17.
Estimates for an evening out.

ENTRY FEES
(for nightclubs & bingo)
£37

CINEMAS
£42

SOCIAL EVENTS &
GATHERINGS
£10

LIVE SHOWS
(including theatre & concerts)
£78

BINGO STAKES
(excluding admission)
£10

DRINKS IN
PUBS & BARS
£412

# THE GREAT BRITISH GETAWAY

Thomas Cook used to be a staple on the high street, along with a raft of other travel agents. Almost everything they offered was a package holiday with flights and accommodation all thrown in, possibly with some other bits besides. Despite coffee shops taking their spots, the popularity of city breaks and the rise of a host of online options, us Brits still love a package holiday. More than half of our holiday spend was on package holidays, leaving spending elsewhere looking miniscule in comparison.

Figures represent average annual household expenditure, 2016/17.

DOMESTIC FLIGHTS
£10

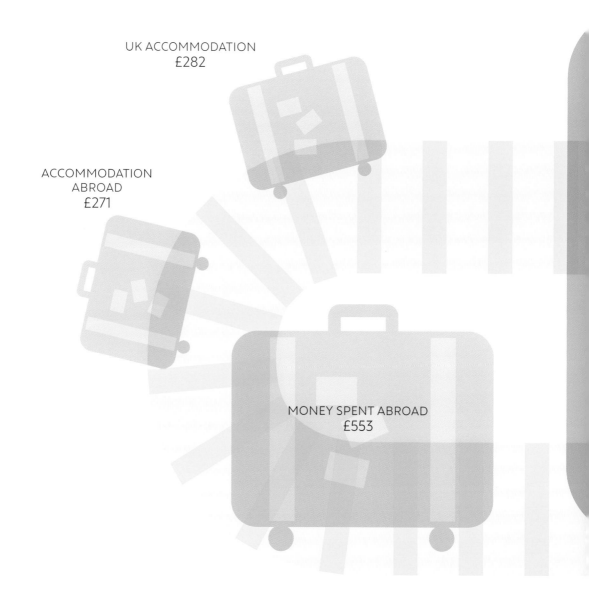

UK ACCOMMODATION
£282

ACCOMMODATION
ABROAD
£271

MONEY SPENT ABROAD
£553

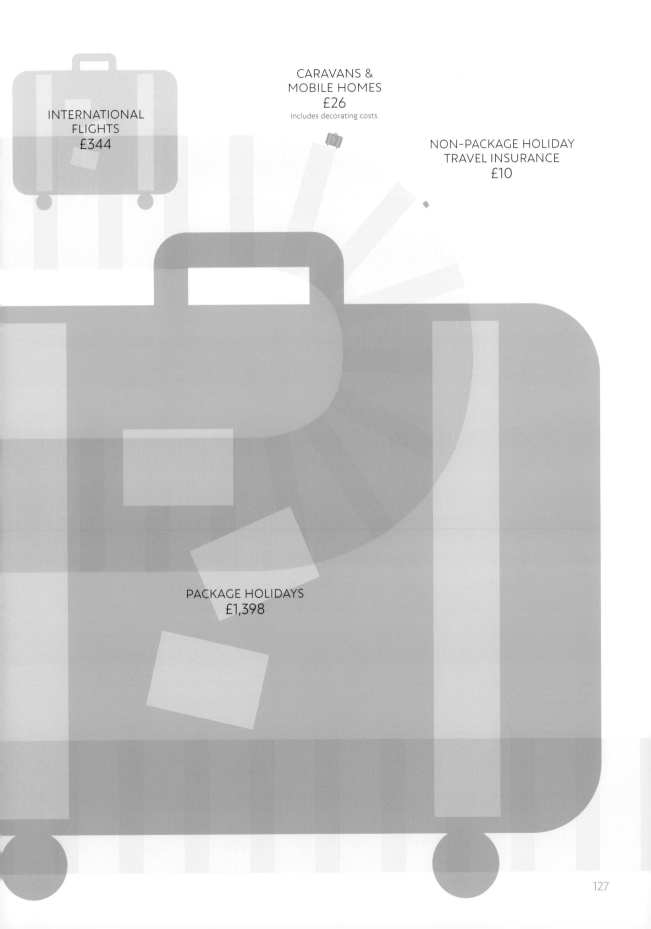

INTERNATIONAL
FLIGHTS
£344

CARAVANS &
MOBILE HOMES
£26
Includes decorating costs.

NON-PACKAGE HOLIDAY
TRAVEL INSURANCE
£10

PACKAGE HOLIDAYS
£1,398

# SPENDING ON THE HOME

For most people, housing is their biggest monthly cost, although it's easy to look at these cogs and think that owning is far cheaper than renting. That is not necessarily the case, as mortgage costs relate only to the interest elements of mortgage payments. The principal element is treated differently in how spending is categorised.

It's also worth remembering that these are averages across households, so while home help costs are low at £16 per year, it's also true that most people do not have this cost. As such, it must be much higher for some. This is also why renting costs are less than £2,000 a year: a large proportion of people don't rent so their rent costs are zero.

Figures represent average annual household expenditure, 2016/17.

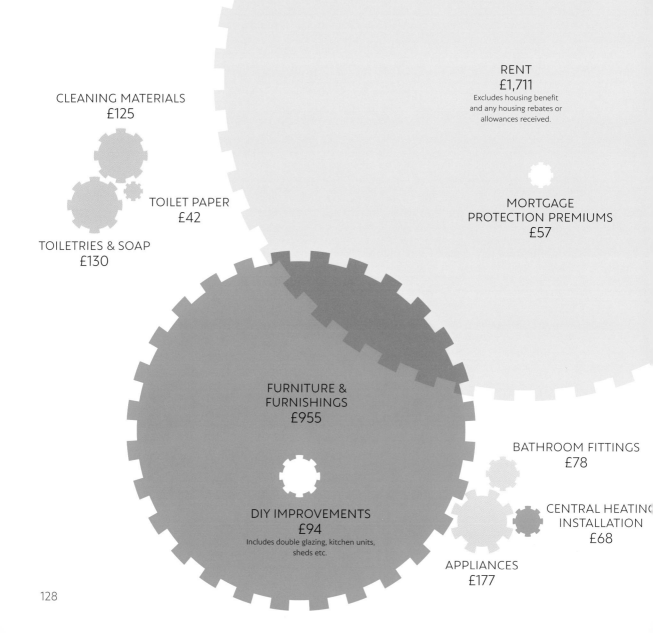

CLEANING MATERIALS
£125

TOILET PAPER
£42

TOILETRIES & SOAP
£130

RENT
£1,711
Excludes housing benefit
and any housing rebates or
allowances received.

MORTGAGE
PROTECTION PREMIUMS
£57

FURNITURE &
FURNISHINGS
£955

DIY IMPROVEMENTS
£94
Includes double glazing, kitchen units,
sheds etc.

BATHROOM FITTINGS
£78

CENTRAL HEATING
INSTALLATION
£68

APPLIANCES
£177

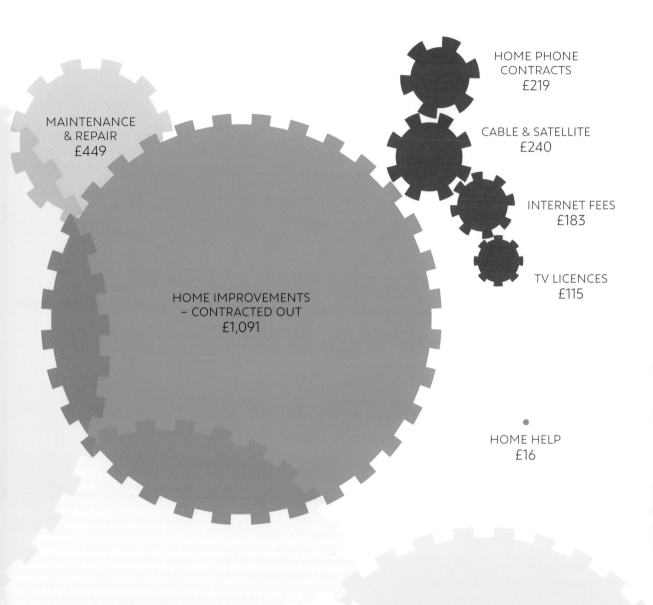

MAINTENANCE
& REPAIR
£449

HOME PHONE
CONTRACTS
£219

CABLE & SATELLITE
£240

INTERNET FEES
£183

TV LICENCES
£115

HOME IMPROVEMENTS
– CONTRACTED OUT
£1,091

HOME HELP
£16

MORTGAGE
INTEREST PAYMENTS
£1,091

HOUSEHOLD
INSURANCES
£250

COUNCIL TAX
& DOMESTIC RATES
£1,169

## HOBBIES AND PASTIMES

If our spending is a reflection of our interests, then British households value sports classes four times more than attending sporting events. And we value gambling more than both. Although in reality our spending is much more a reflection of how much things cost than our collective desire to have them. A flurry at bingo need not cost much, but when lots of households partake it adds up.

We did spend (in 2016/17) about as much on horticultural goods and plants as we did on TVs, videos and computers (videos might seem outdated and out of place on this list, but this does reflect how data categories change at a slower pace to technology – statisticians always have to play catch up...) I guess we're a green-fingered bunch.

Figures represent average annual household expenditure, 2016/17.

## STAYING IN

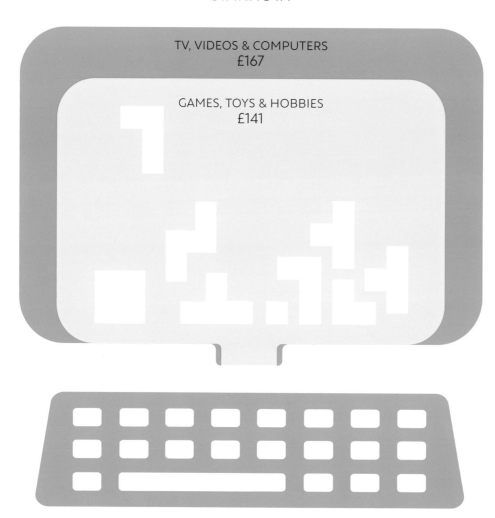

TV, VIDEOS & COMPUTERS
£167

GAMES, TOYS & HOBBIES
£141

SPORTS

HOBBIES
& PASTIMES

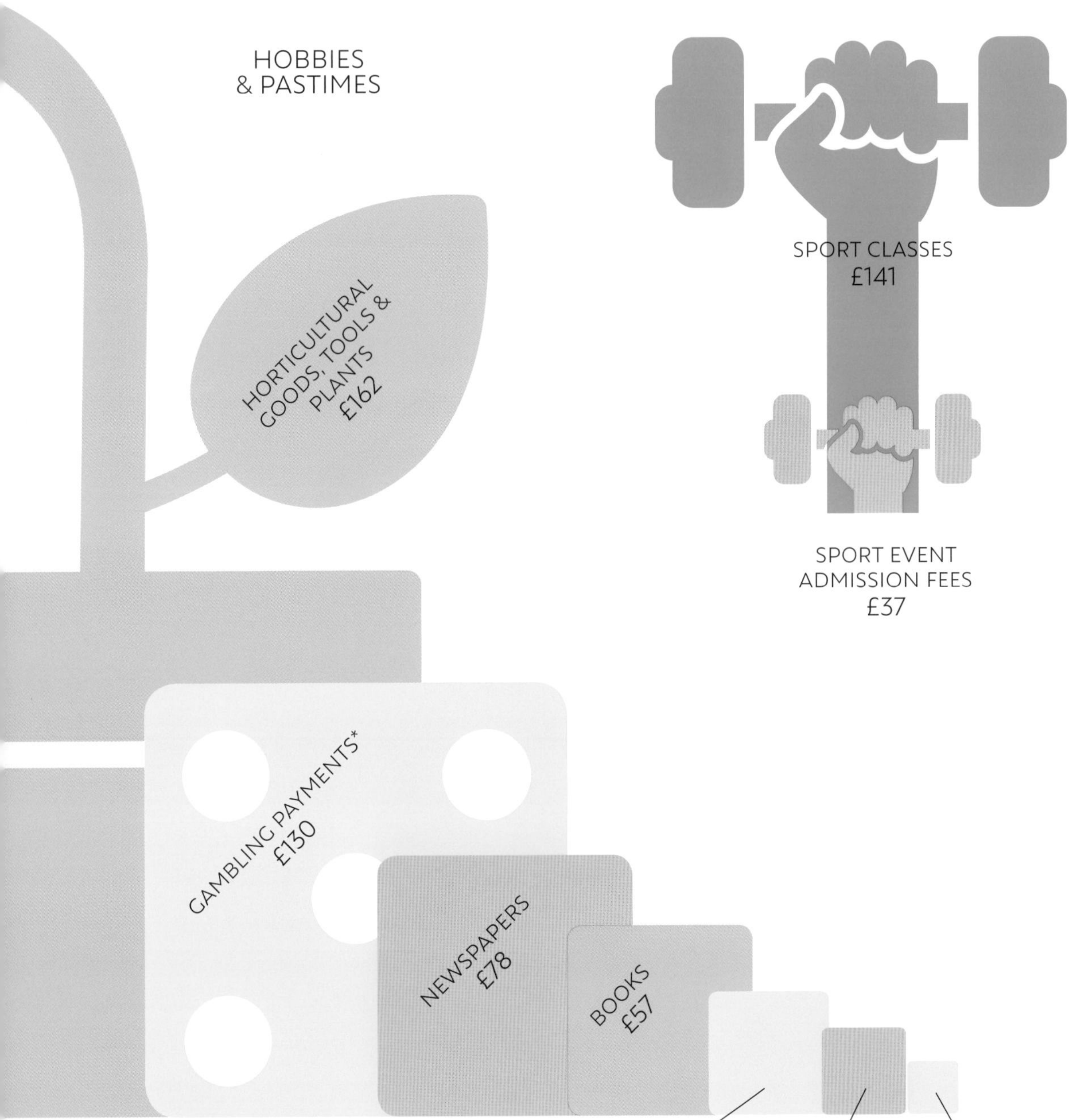

HORTICULTURAL
GOODS, TOOLS &
PLANTS
£162

SPORT CLASSES
£141

SPORT EVENT
ADMISSION FEES
£37

GAMBLING PAYMENTS*
£130

NEWSPAPERS
£78

BOOKS
£57

* Gambling includes bingo
stakes, lottery, bookmaker
& other betting stakes but
excludes winnings, which
are treated as income (these
represent about £73 per
household per year).

MAGAZINES
£37

VISITOR
ATTRACTIONS
£26
Includes museums, zoological
gardens, theme parks, houses
and gardens.

MUSICAL
INSTRUMENTS
£16

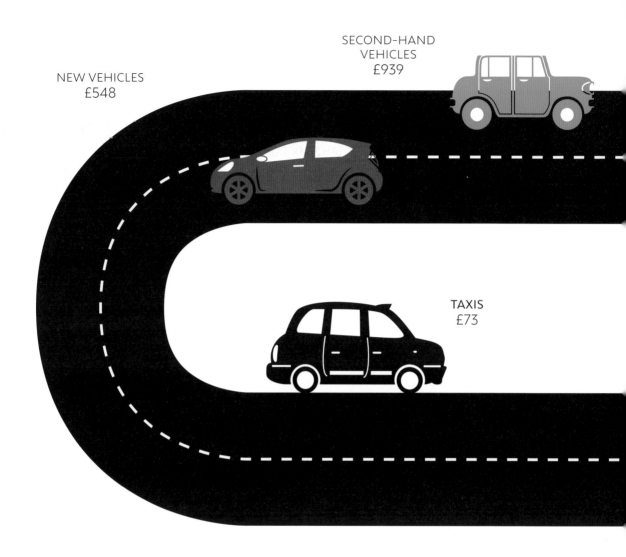

NEW VEHICLES
£548

SECOND-HAND
VEHICLES
£939

TAXIS
£73

BUS & COACH FARES
£73

SPARES & ACCESSORIES
£136

RAIL & TUBE FARES
£198

REPAIRS & SERVICING
£318

CAR LEASING
£183

VEHICLE INSURANCE
£517

## TRANSPORT

After a house, vehicle purchases are often the second largest transactions we make. Such purchases, including second-hand buys, represent more than a third of our total transport costs over a year. No wonder there are so many car ads on TV.

Aside from cars, vans and other private vehicles, household spending on public transport is pretty slim. Just 6p in every pound spent on transport went to public transport in the 2016/17 financial year and this includes taxis. More than half this cost was on train and underground fares, although these figures exclude any non-household spending, including any business travel or net funding from government. Adding these figures would give you national transport costs, which would look a bit different.

Figures represent average annual household expenditure, 2016/17.

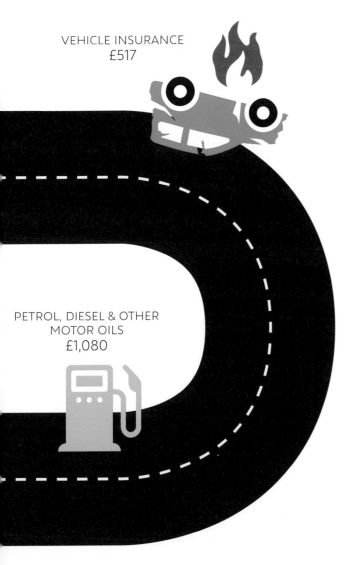

PETROL, DIESEL & OTHER
MOTOR OILS
£1,080

ROAD TAXATION PAYMENTS
LESS REFUNDS
£177

# BILLS AND EVERYDAY COSTS

Our mobile phone bills are, on average, higher than our water bills. Considering water is a necessity, this is either a triumph of human ingenuity in getting the cost of a basic good so low, or a reflection of just how much we 'need' our phones.

Still, both of these costs are tiny when compared with the money that comes off our pay cheques before they go into our banks. To be sure, taxes and pension contributions go towards funding everything our government provides, but it's also true that income tax (which includes all taxes on income minus any refunds) is the largest cost for the average British household.

Figures represent average annual household expenditure, 2016/17.
* Medical costs include optical and dental costs and auxiliary medical products and services.

ELECTRICITY
£579

GAS
£527

WATER
£386

OPTICAL PRODUCTS
£78

PRIVATE MEDICAL
COSTS*
£115

MOBILE CONTRACTS
£391

PRESCRIPTIONS
& MEDICINES
£94

NHS-RELATED
MEDICAL COSTS*
£63

MOBILE HANDSETS
£42

MEDICAL INSURANCE
PREMIUMS
£110

LIFE ASSURANCE
PREMIUMS
£141

VET BILLS
£104

INTEREST
ON CREDIT CARDS
£68

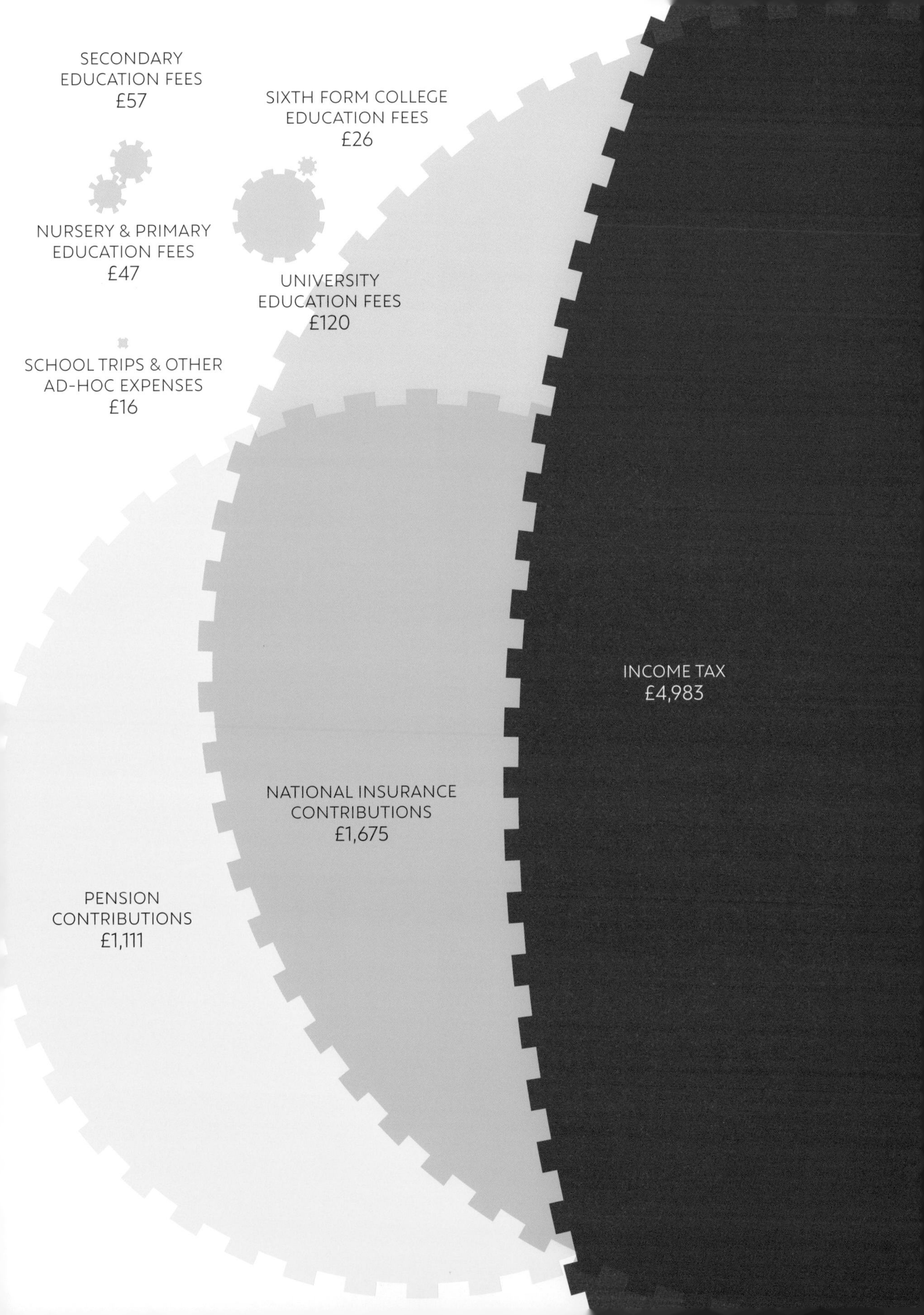

SECONDARY
EDUCATION FEES
£57

SIXTH FORM COLLEGE
EDUCATION FEES
£26

NURSERY & PRIMARY
EDUCATION FEES
£47

UNIVERSITY
EDUCATION FEES
£120

SCHOOL TRIPS & OTHER
AD-HOC EXPENSES
£16

INCOME TAX
£4,983

NATIONAL INSURANCE
CONTRIBUTIONS
£1,675

PENSION
CONTRIBUTIONS
£1,111

# 6

# HEALTH
# AND
# FITNESS

# WHAT WE EAT

Data are collected with an aim in mind. These data were published by Public Health England and the Food Standards Agency and the focus is on health. This can create some categories that are useful for health reasons but may be less useful for other purposes, such as marketing. 'Cereals' relates to breakfast cereals, whereas other cereals and grains, such as rice, are collected with pasta. 'Vegetables' relates only to cooked vegetables with raw veg going with salad. Biscuits, buns, cakes and pastries are all grouped together in 'Buns'.

Furthermore, how data are collected will always have impacts on its accuracy. Like a lot of studies on what we eat, these data rely on diet diaries. When we complete diet diaries, people tend to misreport how much they eat of different foods. This is not necessarily dishonest, but did you really have just two

scoops of ice cream? Were they monster scoops that almost emptied the tub? You might be inclined to think it was just two scoops or maybe there were *two helpings* of veg in that dish.

This survey was paired with physical measurements and blood and urine samples. And the researchers considered energy expenditure to determine how much respondents might have misreported. They used these data to provide information on the accuracy of their estimates, but presented the figures as they were reported. This is better than the alternative of guessing how consumption patterns differed from what was reported.

The important thing is that, with any survey of a topic that carries a value judgement, people will likely be mindful of how their answers are received – somehow heterosexual men always have more sexual partners, on average, than heterosexual women, for example. When it comes to food, it's probably safe to assume we eat a little more cake and chocolate than reported and a little less fruit and veg.

Several categories contain more data than the simplified labels we have used in the image below – see Notes for full details. Data from finanical years 2012/13 to 2016/17.

Age 11–18

Age 65+

Pudding

Ice cream

Eggs

Cheese

Chocolate

Sugar

Sauces

Soup

Savoury snacks

Sweets

Butter

# DISABILITY

The image we use for disabled people is a wheelchair. They're what we paint on parking spaces and they're one reason why buildings have ramps. But this image masks a host of disabilities, from vision and hearing difficulties to mental health or memory loss. And the fact is that as we grow older, we become significantly more prone to suffering a disability, or two, or more. By the time we reach our late 70s approximately half of us will have a disability, and as the UK ages it's likely that the proportion of disabled people will also grow.

Yet disability rates are also increasing on the other end of the age spectrum. To an alien, the data would suggest that some disabilities, such as behavioural and learning disabilities or mental health, afflict younger people more than the elderly. The more obvious answer is that we've found out more about these conditions in recent years. Although there could also be a life expectancy element, where people with certain conditions tend to live shorter lives.

## MALE

| Able-bodied | Disabled | AGE |
|---|---|---|
| 0.5 | 0.7 | 80+ |
| 0.5 | 0.5 | 75–79 |
| 0.8 | 0.5 | 70–74 |
| 1.1 | 0.6 | 65–69 |
| 1.2 | 0.5 | 60–64 |
| 1.5 | 0.6 | 55–59 |
| 1.7 | 0.4 | 50–54 |
| 1.9 | 0.4 | 45–49 |
| 1.8 | 0.3 | 40–44 |
| 1.8 | 0.3 | 35–39 |
| 1.9 | 0.2 | 30–34 |
| 1.9 | 0.2 | 25–29 |
| 1.9 | 0.2 | 20–24 |
| 1.7 | 0.2 | 15–19 |
| 1.5 | 0.2 | 10–14 |
| 1.8 | 0.2 | 5–9 |
| 2 | 0.1 | 0–4 |

2.5    2.0    1.0    1.5    0.5    0.0

MILLION

Aside from age differences, it's important to remember the value that people with disabilities can offer. For example, while the employment rate for disabled people of working age is less than that of the non-disabled, the difference is smaller than you may think. Around half of disabled people work, with 7% being self-employed. Those with disabilities are less likely to work full time, although part-time and self-employment figures are about the same as the general population. There are also similar numbers of retired people, students and unemployed among both populations. The biggest difference between the two groups is the higher number of disabled people who are 'permanently sick/disabled'. But, of course, that's what you'd expect.

Due to small sample sizes, data are an average of financial years 2014/15, 2015/16 and 2016/17. See Notes for details of definition of 'disability'.

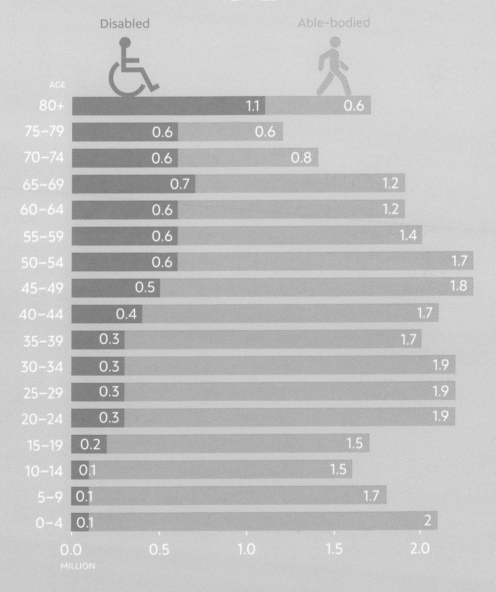

FEMALE

Disabled                    Able-bodied

| AGE | Disabled | Able-bodied |
|---|---|---|
| 80+ | 1.1 | 0.6 |
| 75–79 | 0.6 | 0.6 |
| 70–74 | 0.6 | 0.8 |
| 65–69 | 0.7 | 1.2 |
| 60–64 | 0.6 | 1.2 |
| 55–59 | 0.6 | 1.4 |
| 50–54 | 0.6 | 1.7 |
| 45–49 | 0.5 | 1.8 |
| 40–44 | 0.4 | 1.7 |
| 35–39 | 0.3 | 1.7 |
| 30–34 | 0.3 | 1.9 |
| 25–29 | 0.3 | 1.9 |
| 20–24 | 0.3 | 1.9 |
| 15–19 | 0.2 | 1.5 |
| 10–14 | 0.1 | 1.5 |
| 5–9 | 0.1 | 1.7 |
| 0–4 | 0.1 | 2 |

0.0    0.5    1.0    1.5    2.0    2.5

MILLION

# PHYSICAL ACTIVITY

Do you walk continuously for 10 minutes at least once a week? About 3 in 10 Brits do not. For some, that's understandable. It's harder for some elderly people to hop to the shops and back in the afternoon. But for others it's more concerning. About 1 in 5 Brits in their late 20s/ early 30s don't meet this bar.

But when looking at the data, other elements stand out that are interesting. Men are more than twice as likely to cycle to and from places as women are. This holds for pretty much every age group. Then there's sport. You're more likely to do any kind of sport if you're rich or have letters behind your name. Presumably the higher wage leads to more time and ability to engage in a range of activities (some sports are expensive) and possibly more need to get away from a desk. If the causation was the other way around then we could all lift weights to a higher wage.

Data from 2014. Walking (and cycling) refers to walking (cycling) for at least 10 minutes to get somewhere. The other categories also refer to at least 10 minutes of continuous activity.

**73%**

**70%**

 Higher education (includes diplomas, degrees & above)

 Further education (includes A levels & equivalent qualifications)

Secondary education or below

**68%**

WALKING

142

**70%**

WHICH OF THESE
FORMS OF EXERCISE DID
YOU DO IN THE PAST WEEK?

**34%**

**11%**

**57%**

**27%**

**8%**

**39%**

**17%**

**6%**

CYCLING

AEROBIC SPORT

WEIGHT LIFTING

# EXERCISE

European-wide surveys go across borders – different peoples, cultures and languages. The latter is responsible for some quite clumsy phrasing. These data reflect the 'time spent on health-enhancing (non-work-related) aerobic physical activity (in minutes per week)' from the European Health Interview Survey.

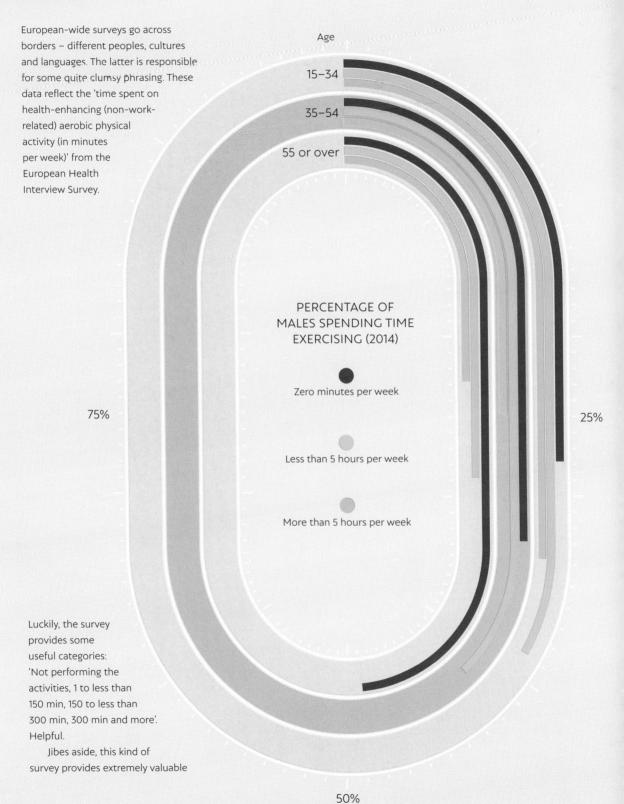

Age

15–34

35–54

55 or over

PERCENTAGE OF
MALES SPENDING TIME
EXERCISING (2014)

● Zero minutes per week

● Less than 5 hours per week

● More than 5 hours per week

75%

25%

50%

Luckily, the survey provides some useful categories: 'Not performing the activities, 1 to less than 150 min, 150 to less than 300 min, 300 min and more'. Helpful.

Jibes aside, this kind of survey provides extremely valuable

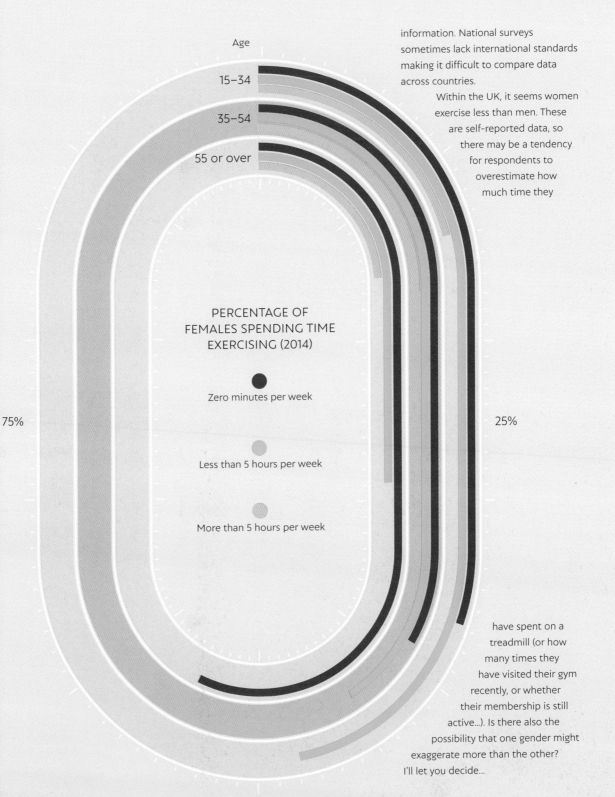

Age

15–34

35–54

55 or over

information. National surveys sometimes lack international standards making it difficult to compare data across countries.

Within the UK, it seems women exercise less than men. These are self-reported data, so there may be a tendency for respondents to overestimate how much time they

PERCENTAGE OF
FEMALES SPENDING TIME
EXERCISING (2014)

● Zero minutes per week

● Less than 5 hours per week

● More than 5 hours per week

75%

25%

have spent on a treadmill (or how many times they have visited their gym recently, or whether their membership is still active...). Is there also the possibility that one gender might exaggerate more than the other? I'll let you decide...

50%

# DRINKING BY INCOME

Teetotal

Had a drink last week

**Under £10,000**
- 28%
- 46%

**£20,000–£30,000**
- 16%
- 60%

**Over £40,000**
- 6%
- 79%

# GO FOR A DRINK LAST WEEK?

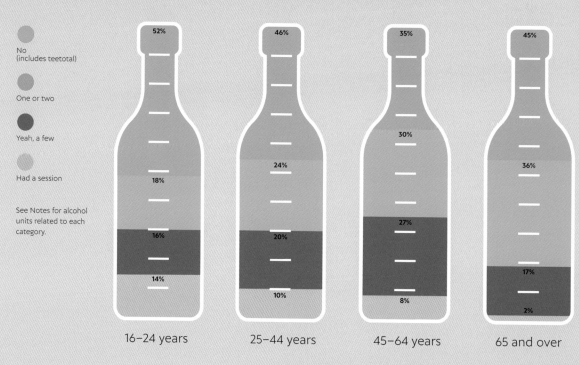

No (includes teetotal)

One or two

Yeah, a few

Had a session

See Notes for alcohol units related to each category.

**16–24 years**
- 52%
- 18%
- 16%
- 14%

**25–44 years**
- 46%
- 24%
- 20%
- 10%

**45–64 years**
- 35%
- 30%
- 27%
- 8%

**65 and over**
- 45%
- 36%
- 17%
- 2%

# DRINKING HABITS

High earners are more likely to drink regularly than those on lower incomes. There's an intuitive element to this: richer people can afford more alcohol, so of course they would drink more. But that is misleading. It's also true that those on higher incomes can afford more cigarettes, but on average, people smoke less as you move up the income brackets.

Social norms play a big part in this. It's socially acceptable (maybe expected) in certain circles to drink regularly. And to drink more, as higher earners are more likely to have a session when they do indulge. On the other end of the spectrum, those on lower incomes are more likely to be teetotal.

There's a further element that some might raise, which is education on the perils of alcohol. We've been told all about the harmful effects of smoking and because income correlates so well with education, you might think that more education will lead to people smoking less. If that is the case (and there's reason to be sceptical), then maybe more information about the health effects of regular and/or heavy drinking would have the same results.

Data from 2017 and only for Great Britain – excludes Northern Ireland.

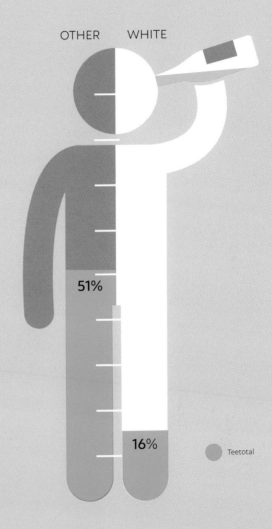

OTHER    WHITE

51%

16%

Teetotal

## DRINKING BY ETHNICITY

There's one other interesting characteristic that determines whether you're more likely to have had a drink in the last week and less likely to be teetotal: if you're white.

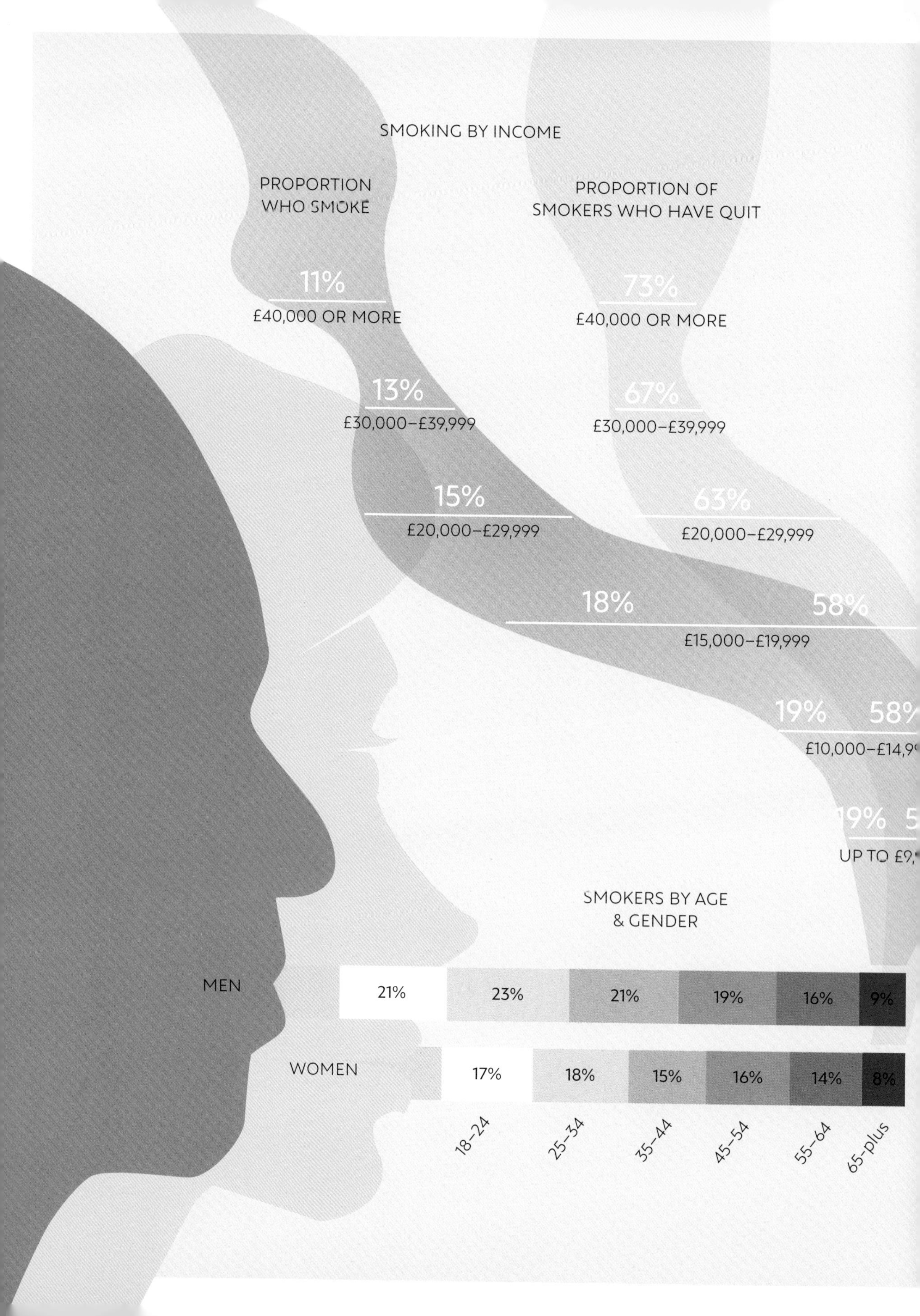

# SMOKING BY INCOME

## PROPORTION WHO SMOKE

**11%**
£40,000 OR MORE

**13%**
£30,000–£39,999

**15%**
£20,000–£29,999

**18%**
£15,000–£19,999

**19%**
£10,000–£14,9

**19%**
UP TO £9,

## PROPORTION OF SMOKERS WHO HAVE QUIT

**73%**
£40,000 OR MORE

**67%**
£30,000–£39,999

**63%**
£20,000–£29,999

**58%**

**58%**

**5**

## SMOKERS BY AGE & GENDER

| | 18–24 | 25–34 | 35–44 | 45–54 | 55–64 | 65-plus |
|---|---|---|---|---|---|---|
| **MEN** | 21% | 23% | 21% | 19% | 16% | 9% |
| **WOMEN** | 17% | 18% | 15% | 16% | 14% | 8% |

# SMOKING HABITS

In the mid-1970s almost half of us smoked. We've since seen a host of laws introduced around cigarette advertising, packaging, where you can smoke and so on. All of this has likely contributed to a steady decline in the number of smokers, helped along by increased awareness of what smoking does to our health.

Yet lots of us still smoke. Those who do are more likely to be men and they're more likely to be less educated and on a lower salary. It's easy to draw causal conclusions from these facts, but this may just be a case of correlation. Whether you smoke might have more to do with whether your parents smoked and your cultural surroundings. After all, as shown on the previous page, those with degrees and high salaries are far more likely to drink. Vice, it seems, cuts across class lines.

Data from 2016 and only for those aged 16 and over living in Great Britain – excludes Northern Ireland.

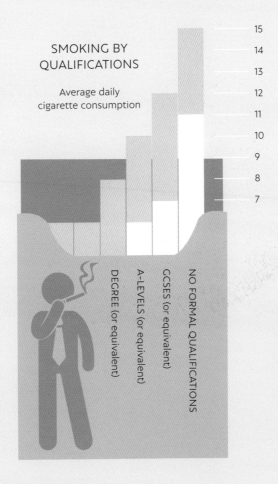

SMOKING BY QUALIFICATIONS

Average daily cigarette consumption

DEGREE (or equivalent)

A-LEVELS (or equivalent)

GCSES (or equivalent)

NO FORMAL QUALIFICATIONS

7
8
9
10
11
12
13
14
15

# DEATHS BY DISEASE

164,400 Cancer (includes various kinds)

## DEATHS BELOW 2,000

- **1,600** Perinatal period deaths
- **1,300** Blood-related diseases*
- **1,100** Rheumatoid arthritis*
- **800** Alcohol-related mental disorders
- **400** Influenza (including swine flu)
- **300** Hepatitis*
- **300** Tuberculosis
- **200** HIV
- **100** Sudden infant death syndrome
- **34** Childbirth-related deaths of mother

69,500 Coronary heart disease

52,400 Dementia

40,100 Cerebrovascular diseases (sometimes causing stroke)

36,200 Chronic lower respiratory diseases (including asthma)

31,900 Pneumonia

24,200 Non-coronary heart disease

16,500 Alzheimer's disease

7,600 Chronic liver disease

6,500 Diabetes

6,100 Parkinson disease

4,700 Kidney-related diseases*

3,800 Tumours*

2,100 Stomach ulcers*

2,100 Skin-related diseases*

2,000 Birth defect-related deaths

# KILLER DISEASES

When looking at the diseases that kill Brits, it's easy to conclude that cancer is the biggest killer. Yet the National Cancer Institute notes that cancer is a name that is given to a collection of related diseases. So if each type of cancer is a different disease then surely coronary heart disease is the biggest killer? But this can be broken down by type as well. This is the difficulty with classifying anything – the details are often tricky.

But the details are important. They determine what gets funding and where we should focus our attention. And it's clear that certain diseases or groups of diseases are top of the list of killers. We may not recognise their medical names (I learned about neoplasms when putting this page together), but we certainly recognise their effects.

Data from 2015.
* See Notes for specifics related to these diseases.

## DEATHS BY CANCER TYPE

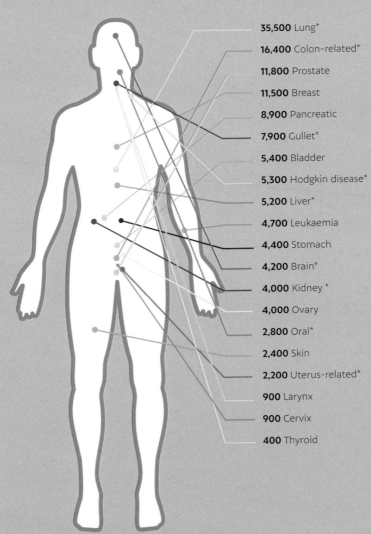

**35,500** Lung*

**16,400** Colon-related*

**11,800** Prostate

**11,500** Breast

**8,900** Pancreatic

**7,900** Gullet*

**5,400** Bladder

**5,300** Hodgkin disease*

**5,200** Liver*

**4,700** Leukaemia

**4,400** Stomach

**4,200** Brain*

**4,000** Kidney *

**4,000** Ovary

**2,800** Oral*

**2,400** Skin

**2,200** Uterus-related*

**900** Larynx

**900** Cervix

**400** Thyroid

# SUICIDE

In the early 1980s, a little over one-third of all suicides were by women. From 1988, that figure has consistently been below 30% and from the early 1990s it has bounced around 25%.

As suggested by this trend, the number of women ending their own lives has stayed relatively stable (close to 1,500 a year) since the early 1990s after falling from around 2,500 a year at the start of the 1980s. The pattern for male suicides is much more erratic, dipping below 4,100 a year in 1982, 1983 and 2007, while topping 4,800 a year in 1988, 1998 and 2013.

Despite these shifts for men, the rate of suicide has remained relatively stable, around 17 in every 100,000 people committed suicide in both decades featured in the stats on this page. For women, the rate has fallen from a high of 11 per 100,000 in 1981 to around 5 per 100,000 in 2017. The decline in suicide rates for women leaves hope that we can reduce these numbers further, although the data since the 1990s suggests that this is a tough battle to win.

Figures are for persons aged 10 years and over. Further details are provided in the Notes.

## PROPORTION OF SUICIDE DEATHS BY METHOD, 2017

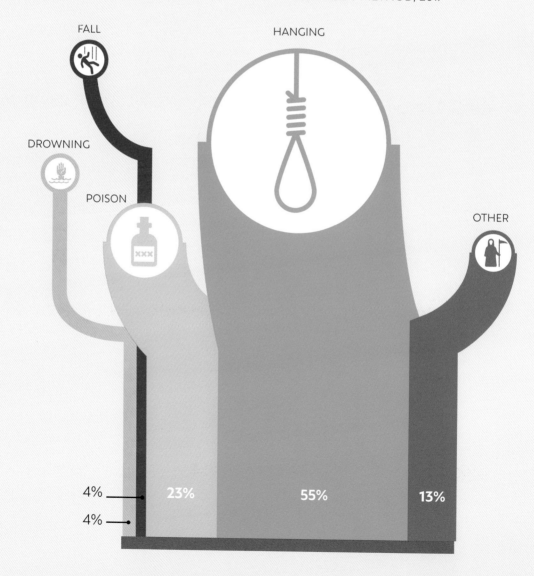

FALL

HANGING

DROWNING

POISON

OTHER

4% ——

23%  55%  13%

4% ——

# SUICIDE BY AGE, 1998–2017

## MALE

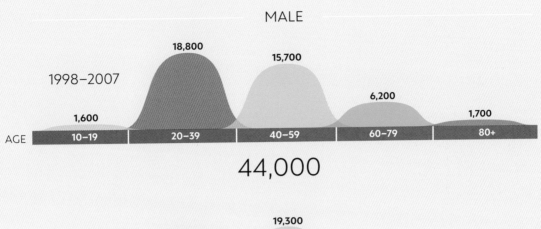

1998–2007

1,600 — 10–19
18,800 — 20–39
15,700 — 40–59
6,200 — 60–79
1,700 — 80+

**44,000**

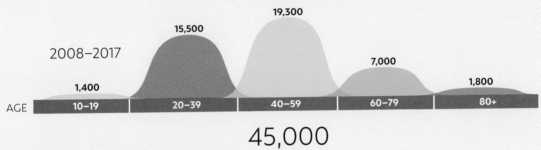

2008–2017

1,400 — 10–19
15,500 — 20–39
19,300 — 40–59
7,000 — 60–79
1,800 — 80+

**45,000**

## FEMALE

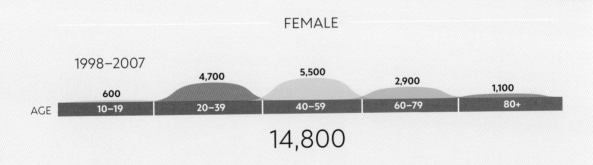

1998–2007

600 — 10–19
4,700 — 20–39
5,500 — 40–59
2,900 — 60–79
1,100 — 80+

**14,800**

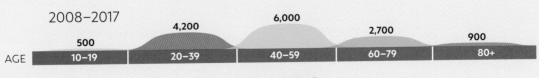

2008–2017

500 — 10–19
4,200 — 20–39
6,000 — 40–59
2,700 — 60–79
900 — 80+

**14,300**

Rounded to the nearest hundred.

# 7

# CRIME

**KIDNAPPING**
2008  2,400
2016  4,200

**ASSAULT**
2008  500,600
2016  470,000

**BURGLARY**
2008  619,100
2016  428,000

**MURDER &
ATTEMPTED MURDER**
2008  1,600
2016  1,100

**CAR THEFT**
2008  161,900
2016  93,900

**ILLEGAL DRUG
TRADING***
2008  40,800
2016  62,400

**RAPE & SEXUAL ASSAULT**
2008  83,500
2016  196,400

Rounded to the nearest hundred.
* See Notes for details of this category of crime.

## REPORTED CRIME

When thinking about how crime has changed over recent years, the data tell some surprising stories. The number of times that certain crimes were reported has sometimes changed markedly, and in some cases has increased markedly. On the positive side, assault, different kinds of theft (including car theft, burglary and robbery) and murder-related crimes have trended downwards. Yet kidnapping is on the up and

drug-related crimes, which tend to trend a little less than other crimes, are also up.

And then there are sex-related crimes: rape, sexual assault and sexual violence. Reports of these crimes have increased significantly in recent years. Yet that may not mean the incidents of these crimes have increased: we have known for years that victims of sexual crimes do not always come forward. This might be related

THEFT & ROBBERY
2008  1,818,400
2016  1,499,700

to feelings of shame, the way they are treated by organisations charged with bringing justice, or the belief that their perpetrator will get away with it either way. The fact that more victims are stepping forward and these crimes are better represented in reported crime statistics is surely a good thing for all victims of sexual crime. And hopefully this is a crime that, like many others, is actually on a downward trend.

Notes
• Where multiple offences are reported, only the most serious offence is logged in England, Wales and Northern Ireland. Also, where one person commits the same offence several times, these countries only log one offence. For both cases, Scotland logs each offence separately, which leads to different results.
• Despite this methodological difference, Scottish data are a relatively small proportion of the total, so the general trend of the data would be unchanged.

# CRIME BY NUMBERS

Crime data, like many social statistics published by government, are collated separately in different countries in the UK. This makes sense because laws (and thus crimes) differ between Scotland, Northern Ireland, and England and Wales. This makes comparisons somewhat tricky: what is included in robbery? There might be a host of things (pickpocketing, burglary, theft...) yet each might have a slightly different definition or recording method. For example, in England, Wales and Northern Ireland, if there are multiple offences, only the most serious is counted. So an assault with theft might appear just as an assault. In Scotland, both are recorded. Still, these numbers give us a neat snapshot of what crime in Britain looks like – and how the nature of the offences we commit is changing.

## 5,489
Number of judges in the UK (2015)

## 1/3
Proportion of judges that are women

## 147,

## 225
Number of police officers per 100,000 people (2016)

## 0.02%
Homicides as a proportion of all reported crimes in the UK in financial year 2017/18

Includes a small number of deaths caused by dangerous driving in Scotland.

## 21,512
Reported obscene publications in England (2017/18)

## 27%
Increase in the occurrence of this offence over a year

Number of reported urinating offences in Scotland (2017/18)

These data recorded as 'Urinating etc'

# 3,044

## 72%

Fall in the occurrence of this offence since 2008/09

Running off without paying - reported cases in Northern Ireland (2017/18)

# 2,363

## 55%

Increase in the occurrence of this offence since 2007/08

Blackmail – reported cases in Wales (2017/18)

# 358

## 34%

Increase in the occurrence of this offence over two years

# 561

**NUMBER OF POLICE OFFICERS IN THE UK (2016)**

# 4,738

Total number of drug-related deaths in the UK (2017/18)

## 36%

Proportion related to heroin and morphine

# 37,759

Personnel numbers in adult prisons (2015)

# COUNTERFEIT CURRENCY

Remember when counterfeit coins were an issue? You don't hear about them as much these days, which partly reflects the cat and mouse game that authorities have to play with criminals. Our pound coins get harder to counterfeit, but criminals still find a way around the new designs.

The latest iteration of this is the new £5 and £10 issued by the Bank of England and printed on polymer rather than paper. The data on this page come from 2016 – the polymer £5 note was issued in September that year with the £10 following in 2017. The Bank has not recorded any counterfeit notes since the updated versions were put into circulation, which is no doubt due to the design of the notes and the difficulty in or cost of counterfeiting them. However, there's probably an even more important element: online crime might be easier and more lucrative than the old-fashioned counterfeiting game. The cat and mouse games continue...

## £1 & £100 NOTES

Unless you're in Scotland or Northern Ireland, it's easy to forget that Bank of England's notes are not the only accepted currency in the UK. Aside from the central bank, there are seven other note issuers: three in Scotland, four in Northern Ireland.

These banks can decide the denominations they choose to issue and six of them issue £50 and £100 notes (Danske Bank has stopped issuing these notes, but at the time of writing they are still in circulation). Danske Bank and First Trust Bank both forgo the £5 note while Royal Bank of Scotland issue a £1 option, making it the only note issuer in the UK to offer six denominations.

250,000

COUNTERFEITS REMOVED FROM CIRCULATION (IN THOUSANDS), 2016, UK

150,000

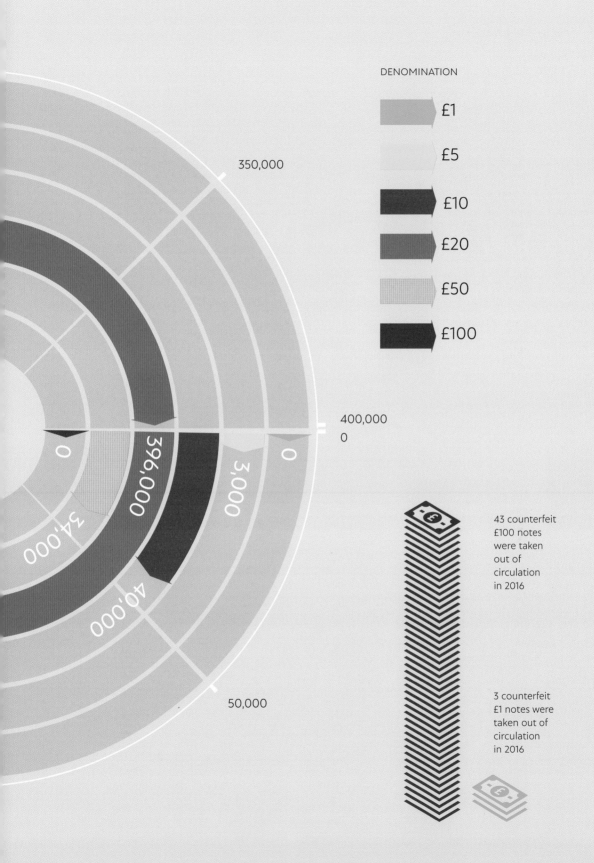

DENOMINATION

£1
£5
£10
£20
£50
£100

350,000

400,000
0

396,000

3,000

54,000

40,000

0

0

50,000

43 counterfeit
£100 notes
were taken
out of
circulation
in 2016

3 counterfeit
£1 notes were
taken out of
circulation
in 2016

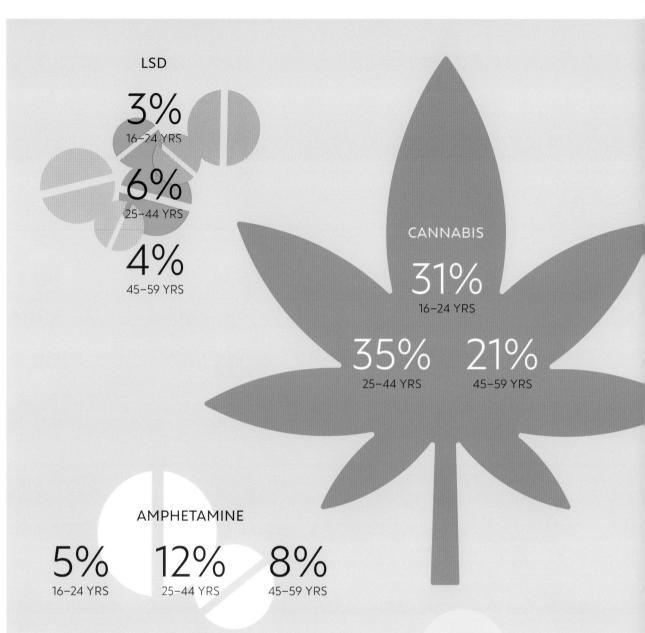

LSD

3%
16–24 YRS

6%
25–44 YRS

4%
45–59 YRS

CANNABIS

31%
16–24 YRS

35%
25–44 YRS

21%
45–59 YRS

AMPHETAMINE

5%
16–24 YRS

12%
25–44 YRS

8%
45–59 YRS

England and Wales data include methamphetamine figures.

1%
16–24 YRS

1%
25–44 YRS

COCAINE (including crack)

10%
16–24 YRS

13%
25–44 YRS

5%
45–59 YRS

ANABOLIC STEROIDS

1%
45–59 YRS

## ANY ILLEGAL DRUG

**35%**
16–24 YRS

**39%**
25–44 YRS

**26%**
45–59 YRS

## METHADONE

**0%**
16–24 YRS

**1%**
25–44 YRS

**0%**
45–59 YRS

Scotland data includes Physeptone figures.

## ECSTASY

**10%**
16–24 YRS

**12%**
25–44 YRS

**4%**
45–59 YRS

**0%**
16–24 YRS

**1%**
45–59 YRS

**1%**
25–44 YRS

HEROIN

## HIGH BRITAIN

From time to time, some otherwise law-abiding Brits will have used certain drugs for non-medical reasons.

Let's get a little more specific: assuming these survey respondents have been entirely honest, 3 out of 10 people have smoked cannabis, which is more than any other illegal drug.

As for the figures on other drugs, there's obviously a large overlap for who's admitting to using different drugs. It has been argued that cannabis is a gateway drug, but the truth is these stats don't tell us. What they do tell us is that only about 1 in 20 people say they've taken some kind of illegal drug but have never dabbled in cannabis. That's about 13% of everyone who admits to taking drugs.

Presumably they took cocaine, amphetamine or ecstasy – the next most popular drugs with about 1 in 10 admitting to taking each of these.

Data from 2014–15. Northern Ireland data include those aged 15 in the 16 to 24 bracket and those aged up to 64 in the 45 to 59 bracket.

## MAGIC MUSHROOMS

**4%**
16–24 YRS

**8%**
25–44 YRS

**6%**
45–59 YRS

# MODERN SLAVERY

Uncovering modern slavery is difficult. It spans countries and nationalities and it comes in various forms. In the UK, we rely on referrals of potential victims to the National Referral Mechanism run by the National Crime Agency. Most of these referrals come from government agencies or the police, although charities and local authorities also submit a notable number of referrals.

In these referrals, there are more British than any other nationality. And most of those referred were male. Both of these facts might jar with the perception of women from Eastern Europe and elsewhere being the most common victims, especially as sex workers. But the numbers on gender are close and it could be that it's easier to unearth male slavery or slavery that involves Brits.

Or maybe our stereotypes are incorrect – the most common referral in 2017 was for adult males exploited for their labour. Either way, referrals for modern slavery highlight that this vicious crime affects a wide range of people, kids as well as adults (more than 4 out of 5 referrals for potential British victims are for children). Recently, the number of referrals has increased year-on-year. This could suggest that the problem is getting worse. Maybe the reliability of referrals is decreasing and many will end up being discounted. Hopefully, it reflects that we're getting better at discovering this crime.

These data reflect referrals to the National Crime Agency – after investigation referrals will be confirmed or rejected as slavery.

## EXPLOITATION REFERRALS BY GENDER, 2017

1,644

810

1,380

1,308

Female adult

Female minor

Male adult

Male minor

# TYPE OF EXPLOITATION REPORTED BY GENDER, 2017

Domestic servitude     Labour exploitation     Sexual exploitation     Unknown exploitation

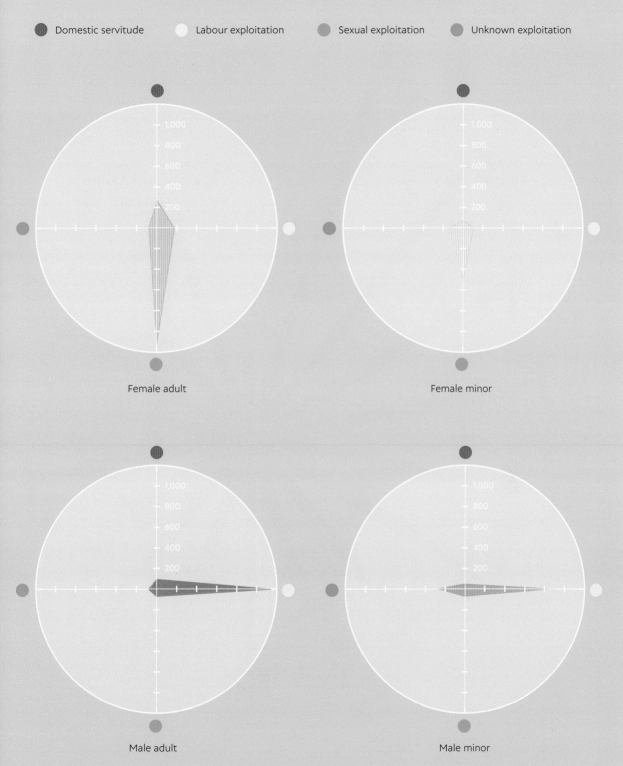

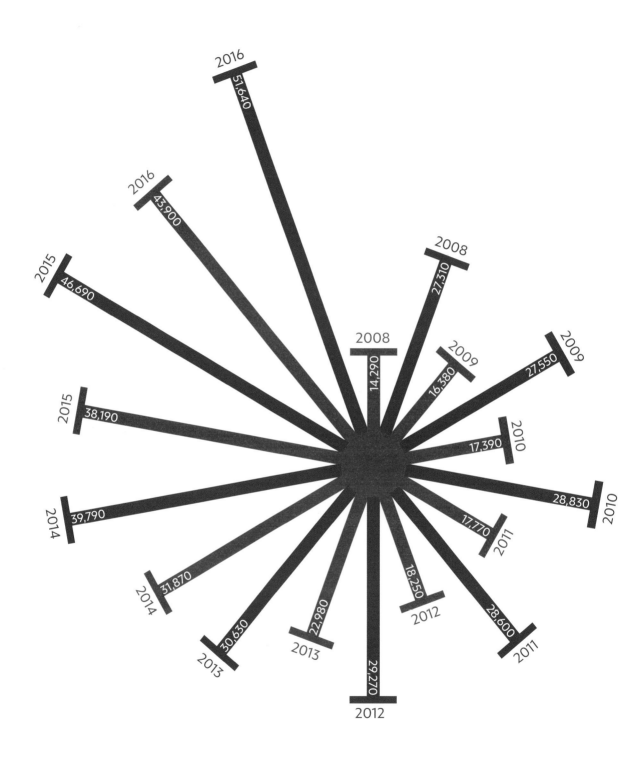

# RAPE AND SEXUAL ASSAULT

Statisticians place a lot of importance on things like data accuracy, reliability and comparability. And these characteristics differ based on how data are collected, by whom and why.

Reports of rape and sexual assault are collected by police forces. But there is another source. The Crime Survey for England and Wales asks respondents about their experience of sexual violence (Scotland has an equivalent called the Scottish Crime and Justice Survey). This is a more reliable estimate of long-term trends as it includes unreported crimes and is independent of police activity and reporting practices. But whereas police reports rely on a legal definition of an offence, these surveys are self-reported, so there can be differences in how people view their experiences of a crime or an event.

Despite possible inconsistencies in reporting, the data provide a different picture to reported crimes: in March 2017 about half a million women and 140,000 men said that they had experienced sexual assault (including rape) in the last year in England and Wales, compared with 65,000 police reports across the UK in 2016. And the rate of sexual assault (i.e. the percentage of the population experiencing this crime) has remained relatively stable since 2005 (at least in England and Wales, which covers almost 90% of the UK population).

So why are the data reported here of any value if crime surveys prove they are under-reporting the extent of this crime? Well the rise in reports is significant in itself because it shows that a higher proportion of sexual assaults and rape are being reported. The increase is thought to be due to improvements in recording practices as well as victims being more willing to come forward (to report recent and past crimes).

The proportion of reported crimes is still woefully low, but the trend at least is positive.

REPORTED VICTIMS, UK

Rape

Sexual assault

Figures rounded to the nearest ten.

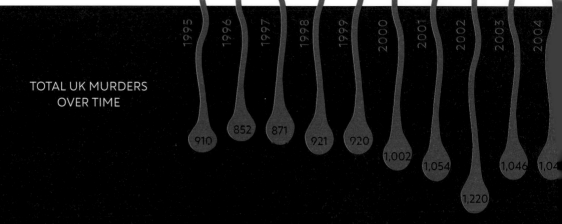

TOTAL UK MURDERS
OVER TIME

910    852    871    921    920    1,002    1,054    1,046    1,04

1,220

## MURDER VICTIMS

There are many possible motives for murder. And these might be
completely detached from any kind of trend. But there are trends in the
number of murders and several factors could contribute to those trends.
For example, the police's capabilities, access to guns and other weapons,
the prevalence or influence of gangs... I've heard fuel emissions being
linked to levels of crime, which seems like a classic spurious correlation.

    Despite trends in the total number of murders, it's important to
consider a few things with these types of data: firstly, the number of
murders is a relatively crude measure and should be considered in line
with population. Although there were more murders in 2016 than in
2008, the population had increased enough that there were 0.3 fewer
murders per million people in the population. It's a small difference, but
it does illustrate how these numbers change when viewed in context.

    Furthermore, the media loves to report on increases in these figures.
But small changes in a short period of time do not necessarily make a
trend. It's important to look at the context of those stories and to see if
they continue over time. And, of course, it helps to look at historical data
to see if any uptick is actually significant.

Younger
than 15
35

25
Younger
than 15

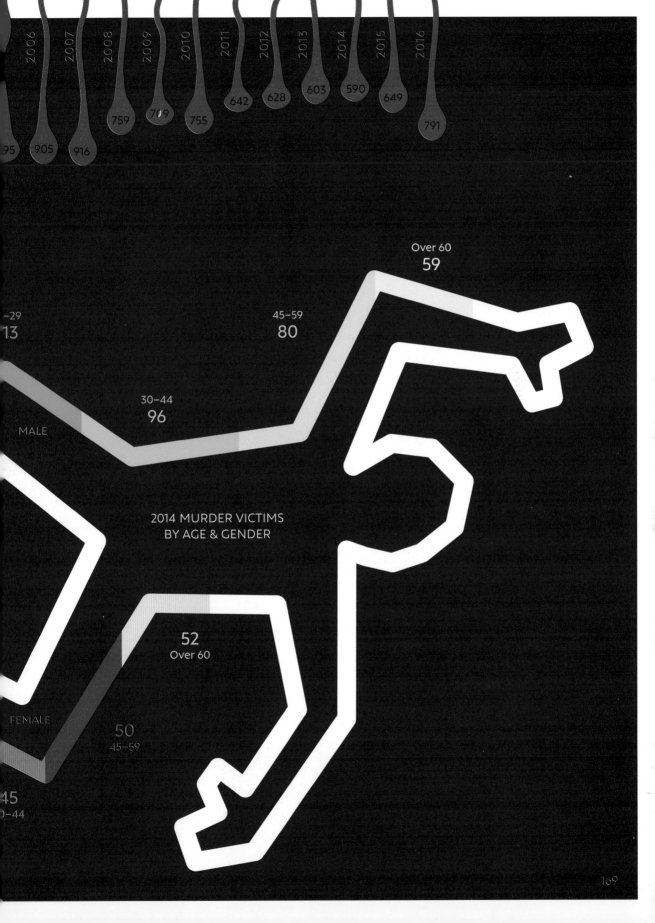

2006 2007 2008 2009 2010 2011 2012 2013 2014 2015 2016

95 905 916 759 709 755 642 628 603 590 649 791

2014 MURDER VICTIMS
BY AGE & GENDER

MALE

–29
13

30–44
96

45–59
80

Over 60
59

FEMALE

45
–44

50
45–59

52
Over 60

# 8

# SOCIETY AND ECONOMICS

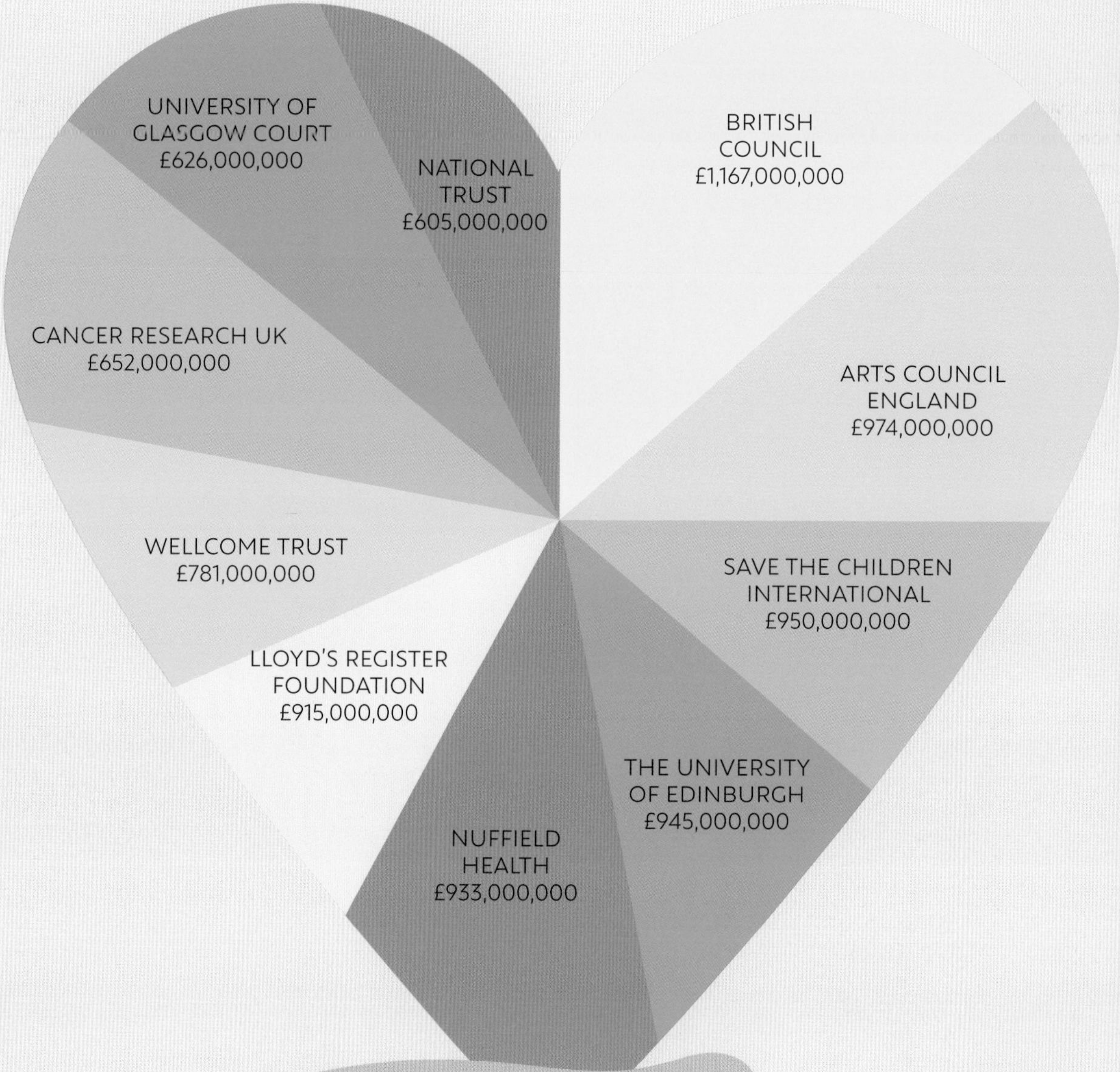

UNIVERSITY OF
GLASGOW COURT
£626,000,000

NATIONAL
TRUST
£605,000,000

BRITISH
COUNCIL
£1,167,000,000

CANCER RESEARCH UK
£652,000,000

ARTS COUNCIL
ENGLAND
£974,000,000

WELLCOME TRUST
£781,000,000

SAVE THE CHILDREN
INTERNATIONAL
£950,000,000

LLOYD'S REGISTER
FOUNDATION
£915,000,000

THE UNIVERSITY
OF EDINBURGH
£945,000,000

NUFFIELD
HEALTH
£933,000,000

LARGEST UK CHARITIES
BY SPENDING
(most recent year or as of February 2019)

England and Wales data as of 23 February 2019; Scottish
data relate to the 'most recent year'; no Northern Ireland
charity had enough spending to make the list.

# CHARITY

Us Brits are a charitable bunch, but the money raised from our sponsored runs and Red Nose Day events pales in comparison with the fees and grants that charities receive for providing their goods and services. This latter element generates more than half of the income for charities in England and Wales. Our giving comes second, although these figures can also include government grants and donations from foundations. Trading comes third, which includes any activity where the donor gets something in return (including charity shops), generating almost 9p for every pound raised.

As such, despite our inclination to give to good causes and to do all manner of challenges and events to raise money, British charities, it seems, are heavily reliant on large organisations to maintain their funding. When these data were collected, that funding led to more than £100 million across 200,000 charities, which could be spent on various causes. Data on charities are collected on a rolling basis, so the numbers are constantly changing.

Data from published annual reports as of February 2019. Data on income and spend breakdown is for England and Wales charities only.

£102,247
CHARITABLE
SPEND
£ (millions)

£105,739
CHARITABLE
INCOME
£ (millions)

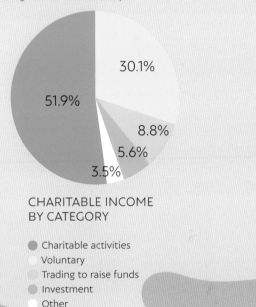

30.1%

51.9%

8.8%

5.6%

3.5%

## CHARITABLE INCOME BY CATEGORY

- Charitable activities
- Voluntary
- Trading to raise funds
- Investment
- Other

1.1%   3.2%

3.4%

0.8%

4.1%

87.4%

## CHARITABLE SPEND BY CATEGORY

- Charitable expenditure
- Generating voluntary income
- Trading to raise funds
- Investment management
- Governance
- Other

# DISPOSABLE HOUSEHOLD INCOME

We all know the difference between salary and take-home pay – you may have noticed those taxes and National Insurance payments nibbling away at your pay cheque. Yet gross disposable household income is more than just our salary minus taxes and social contributions. The Office for National Statistics definition includes all benefits that households receive, e.g. investment income, government benefits such as the state pension, and employers' pension contributions, among other things.

All these data create a useful measure of economic performance. For example, England is the only country where gross disposable household income per person is higher than the UK average. The distribution across England is far from even, and high-income areas have a significant effect on the average.

Then there's the relative success of Scotland over a 20-year period. Although gross disposable household income in Scotland is still below the UK average, it was far closer to that average in 2016 than in 1997. But when comparing relative performance with the average, one country's success mirrors others' poor performance. And in the 20-year period these data cover, Wales lost out relative to the rest of the UK.

Those performances have to be considered alongside price increases, as these data have not been adjusted for inflation. This comparison provides an indication of how relative purchasing power has changed. Inflation over the 20-year period was about 67% (an average of 2.7% a year). Gross disposable household income increased faster than inflation for every country in the UK, but that is not the case for every area.

The West Midlands, West Yorkshire and West Wales all lost purchasing power over the period – that is to say that prices rose higher than their total income. While London and the Highlands both doubled their purchasing power.

However, there are two things to watch out for in these comparisons. Firstly, although we can compare regional incomes, we're only just getting data for regional inflation

## BY COUNTRY

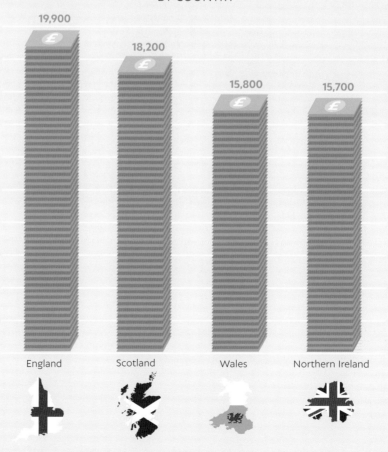

and it's not possible to measure this over the period in question. And differences in price changes between regions could have a big effect on purchasing power.

Secondly, is it the case that things have improved for people in London? Or have successful people (i.e. those that can command a high wage) moved to London? If successful people cluster over time, then the area's relative performance will improve. But the fortunes of those living in London in 1997 might be no better than they were in 2016, wherever they happen to live. And the same can be said if higher earners decide to leave a particular area, making the area look poorer (unless the fortunes improve for their peers who stayed).

Data from 2016. Figures not adjusted for inflation and rounded to the nearest hundred.

## LOCAL CHANGES TO GROSS DISPOSABLE HOUSEHOLD INCOME

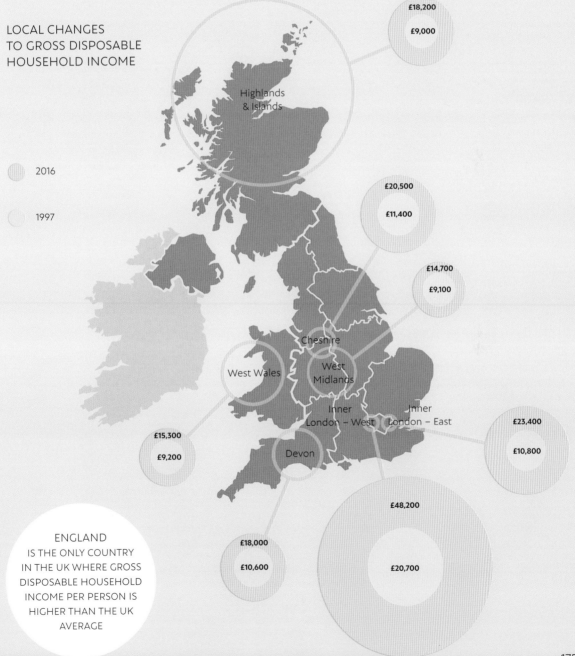

2016

1997

£18,200
£9,000

Highlands & Islands

£20,500
£11,400

£14,700
£9,100

Cheshire

West Wales

West Midlands

Inner London – West

Inner London – East

£23,400
£10,800

£15,300
£9,200

Devon

£48,200

£20,700

ENGLAND IS THE ONLY COUNTRY IN THE UK WHERE GROSS DISPOSABLE HOUSEHOLD INCOME PER PERSON IS HIGHER THAN THE UK AVERAGE

£18,000
£10,600

# HOUSEHOLD DEBT

It's pretty clear that, as house prices rise, our mortgage debt also rises. What's more notable is that total mortgage debt in the UK overtook gross disposable household income in the mid-2000s and has stayed higher ever since.

Gross disposable household income includes a range of things beyond your salary, including investment income and employers' pensions contributions. And because the number of people who have either paid off their mortgage or are renting has increased, this mortgage debt is focused on a smaller proportion of people.

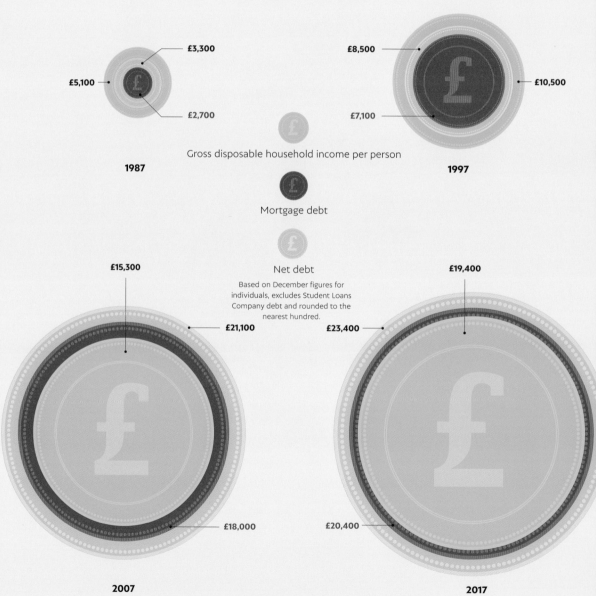

## INDIVIDUAL NET DEBT

£3,300

£5,100

£2,700

£8,500

£10,500

£7,100

Gross disposable household income per person

**1987**

**1997**

Mortgage debt

£15,300

Net debt

£19,400

Based on December figures for individuals, excludes Student Loans Company debt and rounded to the nearest hundred.

£21,100

£23,400

£18,000

£20,400

**2007**

**2017**

# CONSUMER CREDIT OUTSTANDING

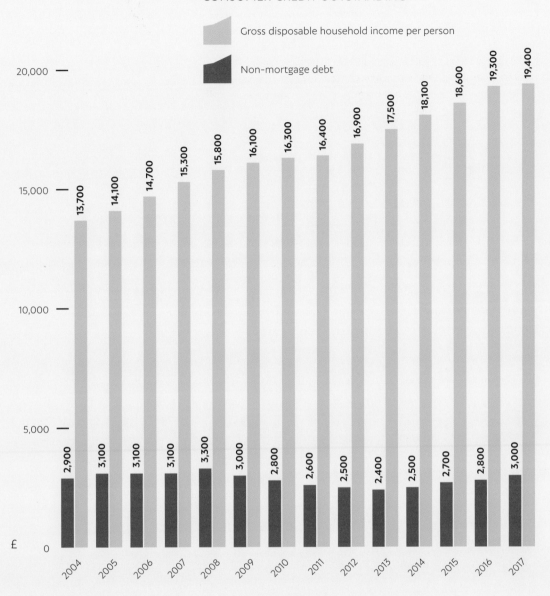

Gross disposable household income per person

Non-mortgage debt

| | 2004 | 2005 | 2006 | 2007 | 2008 | 2009 | 2010 | 2011 | 2012 | 2013 | 2014 | 2015 | 2016 | 2017 |
|---|---|---|---|---|---|---|---|---|---|---|---|---|---|---|
| Gross disposable household income per person | 13,700 | 14,100 | 14,700 | 15,300 | 15,800 | 16,100 | 16,300 | 16,400 | 16,900 | 17,500 | 18,100 | 18,600 | 19,300 | 19,400 |
| Non-mortgage debt | 2,900 | 3,100 | 3,100 | 3,100 | 3,300 | 3,000 | 2,800 | 2,600 | 2,500 | 2,400 | 2,500 | 2,700 | 2,800 | 3,000 |

While the amount of mortgage debt has increased, it's clear that other types of consumer credit have remained relatively stable. This kind of debt includes credit cards, store cards and overdrafts. As wages have grown, this type of debt has become more sustainable. Which is a good thing, as we may need the funds to pay off those mortgages.

# THE INFLATION BASKET

Inflation – the general change in prices over time – is measured by taking a basket of items bought by households and tracking their prices each month. In the UK, we measure over 700 goods and services, tracking their prices in approximately 20,000 outlets, including online stores.

However, in order to stay relevant, the basket is reviewed annually to ensure that the items still reflect what we actually buy. These changes provide insights into how life in Britain has changed over time: our eating habits, fashion choices, hygiene rituals etc. It also provides an excellent take on when different gadgets became important in our lives, as opposed to when they were invented. Overall, it's an interesting look at the way we were and one we rarely consider.

1947

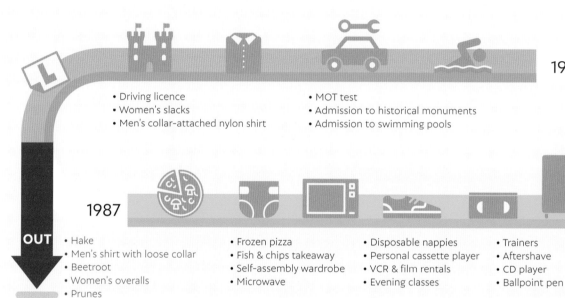

1974

- Driving licence
- Women's slacks
- Men's collar-attached nylon shirt

- MOT test
- Admission to historical monuments
- Admission to swimming pools

1987

**OUT**
- Hake
- Men's shirt with loose collar
- Beetroot
- Women's overalls
- Prunes

- Frozen pizza
- Fish & chips takeaway
- Self-assembly wardrobe
- Microwave

- Disposable nappies
- Personal cassette player
- VCR & film rentals
- Evening classes

- Trainers
- Aftershave
- CD player
- Ballpoint pen

- Mineral water
- Small pet (e.g. hamster)
- Music downloads
- Nursing home fees
- Full leg wax
- Shower gel

- Frozen prawns
- Slimming clubs
- Mobile phone handset
- Nanny fees
- Takeaway coffee

- Laptop computer
- Digital radio
- Air fares
- Organic fruit & vegetables

2015

Portable radio-cassette player •
Disposable razors •
Local newspaper •
Writing paper •
Women's shoe repair •
Annual credit card charges •

**OUT**

- Women's premium branded dress
- Canvas fashion shoe/trainer
- Disposable contact lenses
- Hardback fiction & teenage fiction books
- Tablet computers

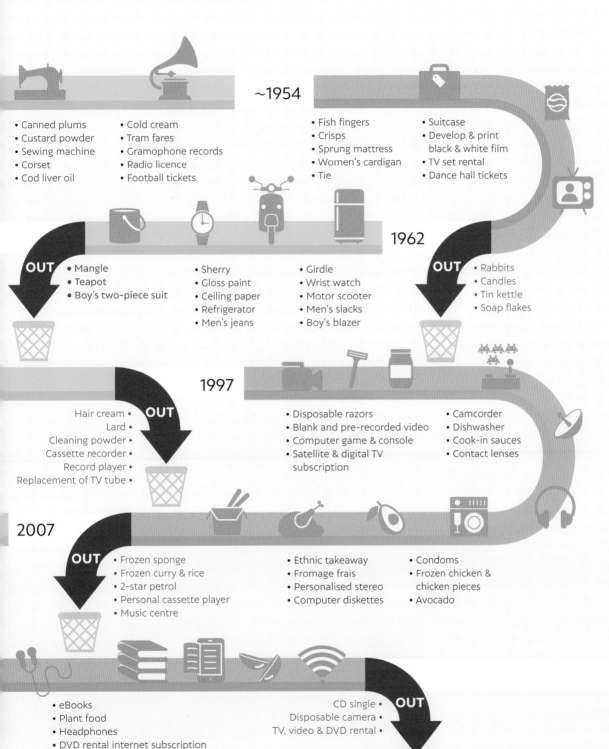

**~1954**

- Canned plums
- Custard powder
- Sewing machine
- Corset
- Cod liver oil
- Cold cream
- Tram fares
- Gramophone records
- Radio licence
- Football tickets

- Fish fingers
- Crisps
- Sprung mattress
- Women's cardigan
- Tie
- Suitcase
- Develop & print black & white film
- TV set rental
- Dance hall tickets

**1962**

**OUT**
- Mangle
- Teapot
- Boy's two-piece suit

- Sherry
- Gloss paint
- Ceiling paper
- Refrigerator
- Men's jeans

- Girdle
- Wrist watch
- Motor scooter
- Men's slacks
- Boy's blazer

**OUT**
- Rabbits
- Candles
- Tin kettle
- Soap flakes

**1997**

**OUT**
- Hair cream
- Lard
- Cleaning powder
- Cassette recorder
- Record player
- Replacement of TV tube

- Disposable razors
- Blank and pre-recorded video
- Computer game & console
- Satellite & digital TV subscription

- Camcorder
- Dishwasher
- Cook-in sauces
- Contact lenses

**2007**

**OUT**
- Frozen sponge
- Frozen curry & rice
- 2-star petrol
- Personal cassette player
- Music centre

- Ethnic takeaway
- Fromage frais
- Personalised stereo
- Computer diskettes

- Condoms
- Frozen chicken & chicken pieces
- Avocado

- eBooks
- Plant food
- Headphones
- DVD rental internet subscription

**OUT**
- CD single
- Disposable camera
- TV, video & DVD rental

# A CUP OF TEA AND A BACON SANDWICH

'The entire British Empire was built on cups of tea,' according to a quote from the movie *Lock, Stock and Two Smoking Barrels*. And given our national drink has been a staple for so long, it's interesting to see how the price has changed. To do so, we need to look at the components of a good cuppa: tea, milk and (for some) sugar. This requires using standard weights for these items and price data, which we have from 1914.

But you can't live on tea alone, so we've added a second British staple: the bacon sandwich.

While it's tempting to imagine these British standards as unchanging over time, the truth is that spending habits and changes in products have had an effect on the basic components of even these national favourites. To create a consistent time series, it's necessary to use unwrapped white bread, ignoring the sliced variety most of us buy. Yet there are some elements that have adapted so much that they've changed our consumption behaviours. The less surprising example is that we've

## THE PRICE OF A CUPPA*

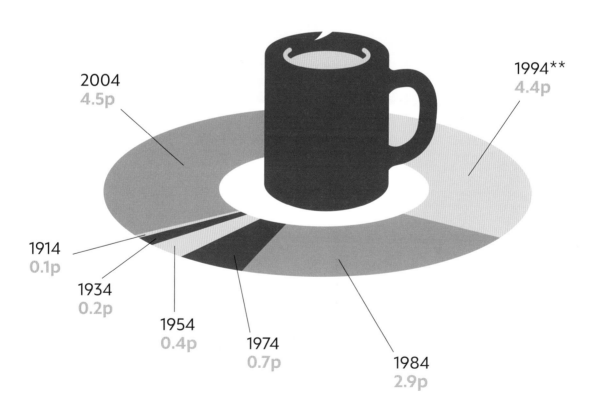

2004
4.5p

1994**
4.4p

1914
0.1p

1934
0.2p

1954
0.4p

1974
0.7p

1984
2.9p

\* Based on 2g of tea (the average for a teabag), a teaspoon of sugar (4g) and 50ml of milk per cup.
\*\* From 1994, 125g equivalent of tea bags replaces 125g of loose-leaf tea.

\* Based on two slices of bread (28g each), 4g of butter and two rashers of bacon (at 25g each).

\*\* From 1974, back bacon replaces streaky bacon, adding 2p to the cost of the sandwich components at that time. The price of back bacon subsequently rises at a faster rate than streaky bacon.

## THE PRICE OF A BACON SARNIE*

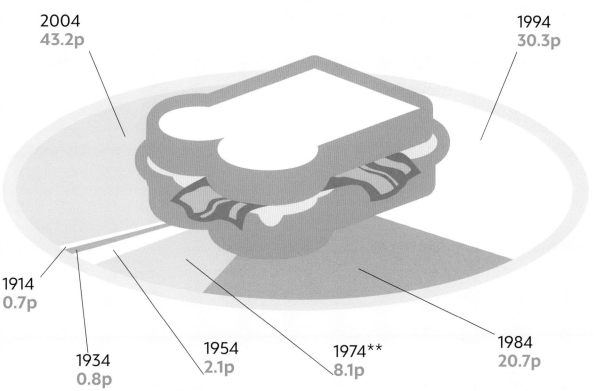

**2004**
**43.2p**

**1994**
**30.3p**

**1914**
**0.7p**

**1934**
**0.8p**

**1954**
**2.1p**

**1974\*\***
**8.1p**

**1984**
**20.7p**

moved from loose tea to tea bags. The latter were included in the Retail Price Index in 1986 and loose tea fell off the list in 2001. The more surprising example is bacon: the streaky kind was the only bacon product whose price was collected from 1914 to 1967. It was later joined by bacon collar, gammon, smoked bacon middle and back bacon. Streaky bacon finally dropped from the price list in 2000, solidifying our ability to look down on Americans for eating inferior bacon.

The other element that is notable from these price changes is that inflation is neither inevitable or consistent. The 1920s and early 1930s saw a tough economic period for the UK, and that came with falls in the general price level (deflation). For our ingredients, the price of everything, except milk, fell from 1924 to 1934. Compare that with the inflationary effects of the 1970s. In recent times, price rises have been the norm, although we have mostly seen small increases year-on-year. Since 1997, it has been an aim of the Bank of England to keep price rises stable, so for the time being it seems unlikely we'll see the kind of erratic price changes notable in the past.

# PUBLIC SECTOR WORKERS

About 17% of employed people worked in the public sector in 2017. But while we all know what 'public sector' means, we rarely consider what it covers.

At the time of writing, the government splits its activities into: 45 departments with ministers (plus the office of the Prime Minister); 405 agencies and other public bodies (these range from arts councils and public museums to policing boards and the Bank of England); 82 'high-profile groups' (including the Border Force, the Office for Disability Issues and groups representing the 25 professions working in government which themselves range from lawyers and intelligence pros to vets); 11 public corporations (the BBC, Ordnance Survey, Civil Aviation Authority etc); and three devolved administrations – each country in the UK, except England, has one.

Then there's local government, which is made up of councils, unitary authorities, metropolitan districts... it might all seem a bit overwhelming.

A simple way to look at it is to ask about the focus of those working for government. In late 2017, health and education dominated in this regard, followed by public administration. About 40% of the latter are civil servants and of these, 1 in 5 (about 83,000 people) worked for the Department for Work and Pensions. HMRC (the tax office) and various justice bodies each employed another 67,000 or so. It's worth considering whether this matches how we prioritise different aspects of life in the UK. It's a difficult question to answer, but an important one to consider nonetheless.

Data from September 2017 (thousands).

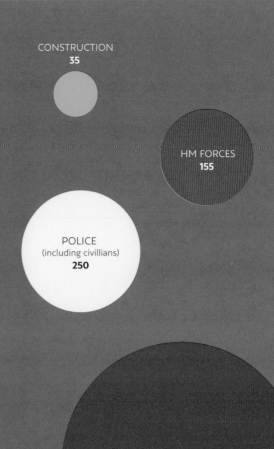

CONSTRUCTION
35

HM FORCES
155

POLICE
(including civillians)
250

PUBLIC ADMINISTRATION
1,017

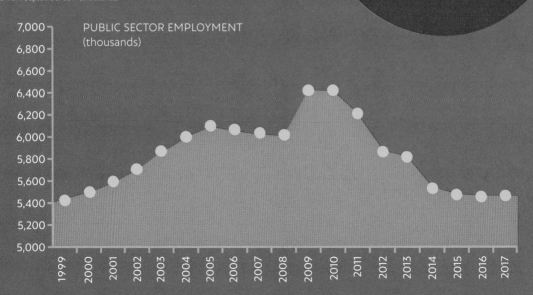

PUBLIC SECTOR EMPLOYMENT
(thousands)

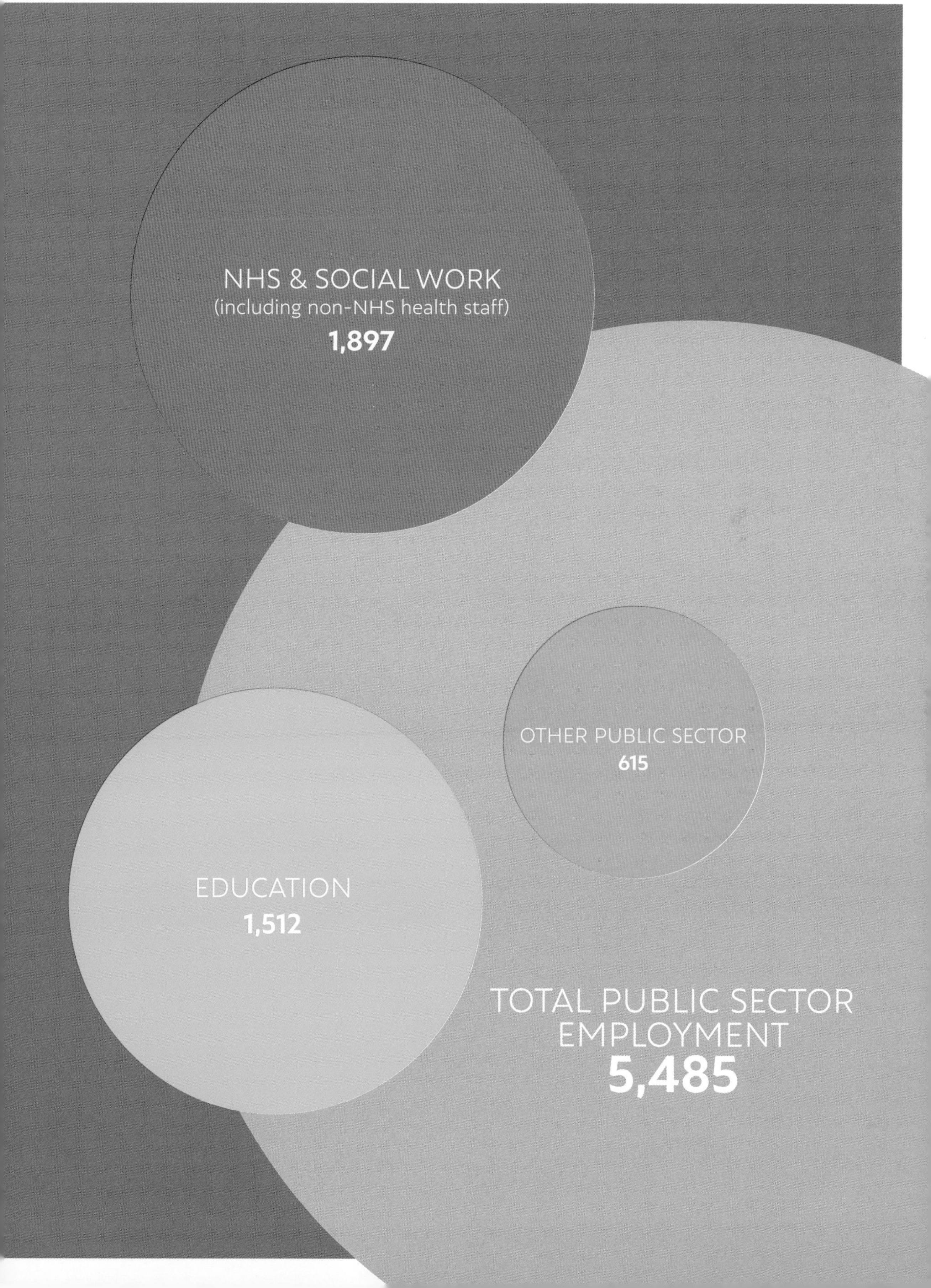

NHS & SOCIAL WORK
(including non-NHS health staff)
**1,897**

OTHER PUBLIC SECTOR
**615**

EDUCATION
**1,512**

TOTAL PUBLIC SECTOR
EMPLOYMENT
**5,485**

# PUBLIC SPENDING

We all have opinions on where the government should spend more or less money. For those in the treasury, priorities have to be assessed, options weighed and decisions made. The outcome – the spending levels the government allocates to different areas – is something we rarely see or assess.

That's a shame because seeing how much we spend on each public service relative to others gives us an appreciation of how difficult these decisions can be and how exercised we should be about different types of spending. Should we spend less on housing than we do on protecting the environment? Is it OK that we spend more on railways than we do on income support and tax credits? Is foreign aid more important than post-secondary education spending?

These are ultimately value judgements, but knowing the figures helps us make the argument. So it's important that these data are public, accessible to and understood by all.

## SPENDING IN CERTAIN AREAS, 2016–17*

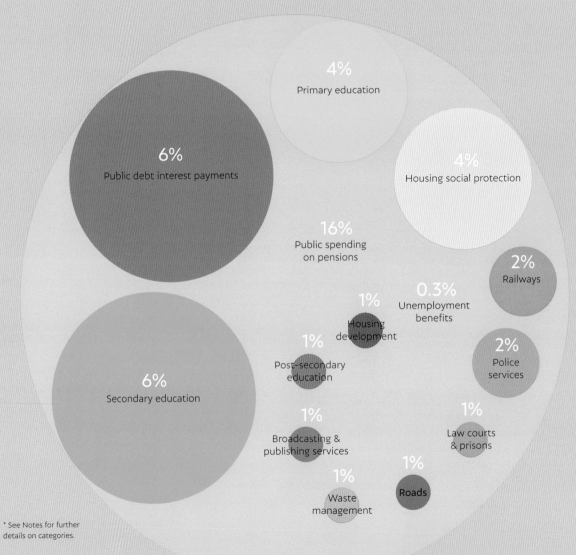

* See Notes for further details on categories.

# TOTAL PUBLIC SPENDING BREAKDOWN, 2016–17*

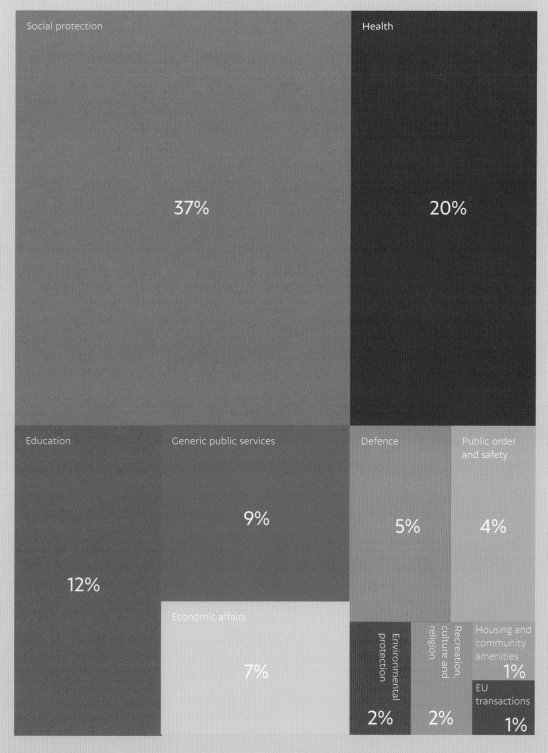

Social protection
37%

Health
20%

Education
12%

Generic public services
9%

Economic affairs
7%

Defence
5%

Public order and safety
4%

Environmental protection
2%

Recreation, culture and religion
2%

Housing and community amenities
1%

EU transactions
1%

# PUBLIC SPENDING GROWTH

Austerity is a charged subject. But what does it actually mean? Critics are swift to point to the fact that the total debt has continued to increase. This, some might say, is testament to the fact that austerity has failed. But there are other ways to look at the matter.

One way is to consider what the government has spent over the long term and how that has changed. Even when taking inflation out of the equation, it's clear that government spending was on an upward trajectory for a long period of time. What austerity did from 2010 was to end that growth. Public spending, in 2017 prices, remained flat from 2010 to 2017. Regardless of your thoughts on austerity, whether it was needed or whether it did the job, changing this trend is a significant feat.

These figures show the trend in public spending on a per person basis between each year ending with '7'. Spending has increased for all of these periods, but it's important to note that there was a large increase in spending following the financial crisis. This was due, in part, to the fact that spending increases in a recession, as the government has to pay additional costs such as unemployment benefits. More importantly for 2008, the financial crisis required the government to save the financial sector. Following the introduction of austerity, spending per person has fallen as the population has continued to grow, while public spending stayed flat.

These factors have led to the growth in spending between 2007 and 2017, but at a slower rate than over any other period covered by these data.

Figures deflated to 2017 prices using the GDP deflator published on 29 June 2018. They are converted to a per person basis using mid-year population estimates.

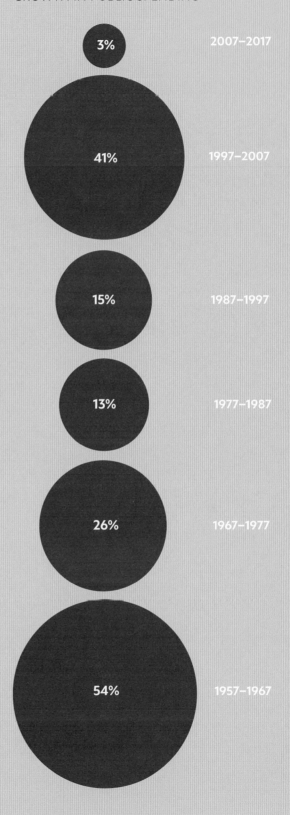

GROWTH IN PUBLIC SPENDING

3%  2007–2017

41%  1997–2007

15%  1987–1997

13%  1977–1987

26%  1967–1977

54%  1957–1967

## PUBLIC SPENDING PER PERSON (2017 PRICES)
Rounded to the nearest hundred.

3,300

5,100

6,400

7,200

8,200

11,500

11,900

£

1957

1967

1977

1987

1997

2007

2017

# REGIONAL GOVERNMENT SPENDING

We all pay taxes and we all receive benefits from the public purse. Yet the distribution of those funds is not equal. Intuitively we know this and we broadly accept that some redistribution of funds has to occur in order to create a more harmonious society. But even though we understand that some individuals pay more into the system or receive more from it, we rarely think about this from a regional perspective.

When splitting the data like this, it's notable that devolved countries (Northern Ireland, Scotland and Wales) are among the top recipients. There could be various reasons for this as certain types of funding might be required. For example, less taxes came from Wales, on average, between 2012 and 2017 than any other region, so spending might have been focused on regeneration or raising skills. This fits a general trend of regions that generate low taxes receive more in spending and vice versa.

Yet there are notable exceptions. Scottish funding is down to an agreed formula and in the years focused on in these pages, it received a higher share of spending, despite being a relatively high contributor to the treasury. London retains a high spot in both camps, which fits with a pattern that the capital is often an exception. By contrast, it would be understandable if those in the West Midlands or Yorkshire and the Humber felt a little hard done by.

Data for average taxes and spending from 2012 to 2017.
Rounded to the nearest hundred.

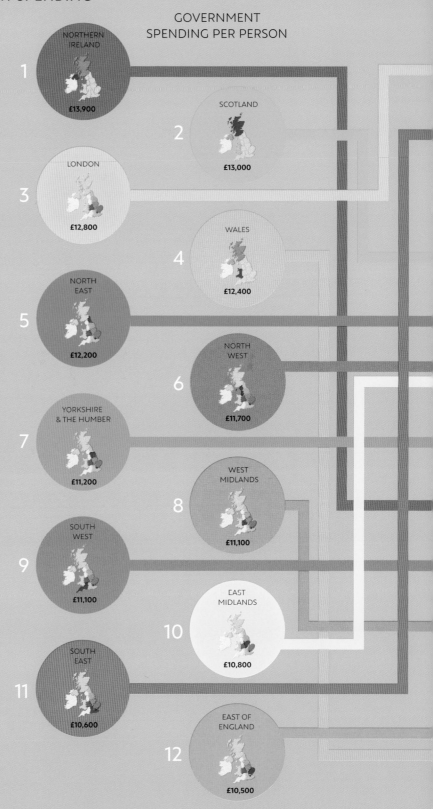

## GOVERNMENT SPENDING PER PERSON

1 NORTHERN IRELAND — £13,900

2 SCOTLAND — £13,000

3 LONDON — £12,800

4 WALES — £12,400

5 NORTH EAST — £12,200

6 NORTH WEST — £11,700

7 YORKSHIRE & THE HUMBER — £11,200

8 WEST MIDLANDS — £11,100

9 SOUTH WEST — £11,100

10 EAST MIDLANDS — £10,800

11 SOUTH EAST — £10,600

12 EAST OF ENGLAND — £10,500

TAXES PAID PER PERSON

LONDON
**£15,100**
1

SOUTH
EAST
**£12,000**
2

EAST OF
ENGLAND
**£10,700**
3

SCOTLAND
**£10,200**
4

SOUTH
WEST
**£9,600**
5

EAST
MIDLANDS
**£8,900**
6

YORKSHIRE
& THE HUMBER
**£8,500**
7

NORTHERN
IRELAND
**£8,500**
8

NORTH
WEST
**£8,500**
9

WEST
MIDLANDS
**£8,400**
10

NORTH
EAST
**£8,100**
11

WALES
**£7,800**
12

## CENTRAL GOVERNMENT TAX REVENUES AND OTHER RECEIPTS
### (£ millions, 2017)

Taxes from household earnings

£322,000

£139,000

£84,000

£72,000

£27,000

£58,000

Business rates

Corporation tax*

VAT

Miscellaneous*

Duties*

# TAX

There are several reasons why the government might tax alcohol. It might want to discourage alcohol consumption. It might want to raise funds to cover any damages from alcohol (including health issues that drinkers might face). Or it might want to raise more revenue. After all, taxes are the government's main source of funds to cover its spending plans.

But when the Chancellor raises taxes on beer or spirits by a few pence here or there, how much effect does it actually have? Just how important is alcohol to overall taxes? These data tell us that duties raised £72 billion in 2017 and alcohol duties made up £12 billion of that figure.

Other duties came from fuel and vehicles, stamp duty, and tobacco.

The breakdown of tax revenue is important because it provides insights into what taxes are important for funding the provision of public services. It also provides a platform from which people can argue for changes in the structure of our tax system. As illustrated above, generating revenue is sometimes only one reason for raising a tax and there might be important consequences to changing tax rates. But the revenue raised is an important element and knowledge of tax and receipt levels is an important step to making a case for change. Or for fighting for the status quo.

* See Notes for details of which taxes are included in these categories.

LOCAL GOVERNMENT TAXES AND RECEIPTS
(£ millions, 2017)

Transfers with public sector*

£112,000

£32,000    £28,000

Other reciepts* £2,000

Pension contributions £3,000

Revenues from public goods and services

Council tax

# GOVERNMENT DEBT AND BORROWING

Government debt is how much the government owes. We all get that part. Then there's the deficit, which relates to its cash flow. If the government spends more than it brings in from taxes and duties, then it has a deficit and has to borrow to fund its spending. If the government spends less than those taxes and related bits and bobs, then it's in surplus and it can pay some back.

The confusing part is how we relate this to the government's ability to pay. If you or I want to take out a loan, the bank would consider our income, the level of debt and our monthly repayments. So our income to loan ratio is an important measure. But those lending to the state focus on economic activity as measured by gross domestic product (GDP). For them, the debt and deficit to GDP ratio is the important measure.

The UK's debt reached as much as 2.5 times its total economic activity after the Napoleonic wars, but in more recent times debt has been closer to 40% of GDP, as it was from the early 1990s to 2008. Since the financial crisis we've seen higher levels – it was hovering

around 88% in early 2018. It reached such heights due to large deficits following the financial crisis. This should be expected as the amount the government gets in taxes falls in a recession because people lose their jobs and companies make less profit. Add to that the additional spending for unemployment benefits and you get higher deficits. In the financial crisis, you also had the risk of bank failures and the subsequent bail-outs increased the deficit even further.

Converted to 2017 prices using the GDP deflator published on 29 June 2018. Debt per person calculated using mid-year population estimates for each year.

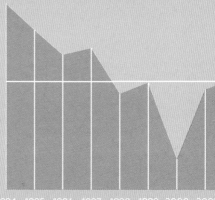

1994  1995  1996  1997  1998  1999  2000  2001

## GOVERNMENT BORROWING
## & DEBT LEVELS

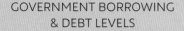

£bn

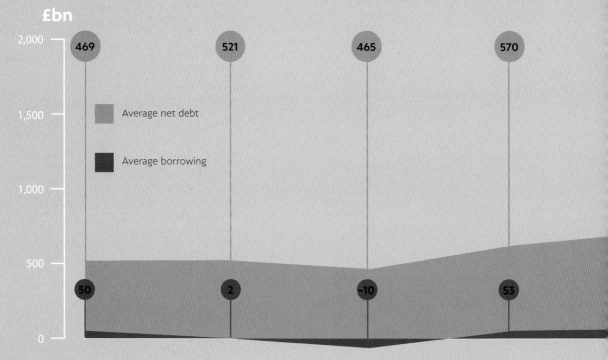

- Average net debt
- Average borrowing

| | 469 | 521 | 465 | 570 |
|---|---|---|---|---|
| | 50 | 2 | -10 | 53 |
| | 1994–96 | 1997–99 | 2000–02 | 2003–05 |

CHANGE IN GOVERNMENT DEBT PER PERSON

£ 3,500
3,000
2,500
2,000
1,500
1,000
500
0
-500
-1,000
-1,500

2002 2003 2004 2005 2006 2007 2008 2009 2010 2011 2012 2013 2014 2015 2016 2017

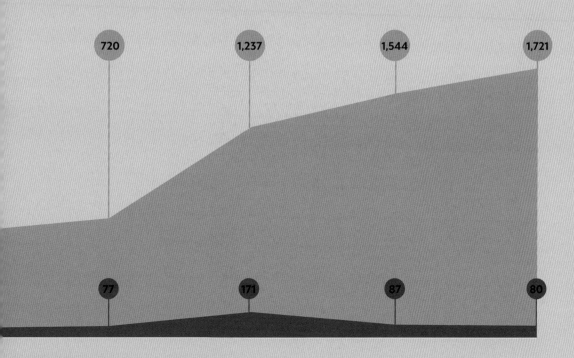

720    1,237    1,544    1,721

77    171    87    80

2006–08    2009–11    2012–14    2015–17

# BRITAIN IN THE WORLD

The UK has a lot of influence in the world. Some of this comes from our wealth, some from our history and some from more recent actions, from involvement in wars to our openness to international companies (this may seem normal to some Brits, but many countries are far less open in their economic engagement than the UK). When considering the interactions of these statistics, they imply a sense of power: ranked 22nd in terms of population, yet 5th richest country in the world; 0.9% of the world population, but 2.4% of billionaires are from these shores. It's easy to see issues behind these numbers (the number of billionaires suggests income disparity, for example), but it's also true that the UK has the means to progress into a bright future.

## 24
UK rank for economic activity per person
(2017)

## £8,009
**WORLD ECONOMIC ACTIVITY PER PERSON (2017)**

Based on author calculations using purchasing power parity statistics.

## £29,

## 5th
Largest economy in the world
(2017)

## 22
Population rank of the UK (2017)

## 1 of 5
Countries with permanent UN Security Council membership

# 3%

Total proportion of the world's migrants living in the UK (2017)

# 11%

Total proportion of Europe's migrants living in the UK (2017)

# 0.9%

UK population as a proportion of the world population (2018)

# 9%

UK population as a proportion of Europe's population (2018)

# 63.5%

UK population as a proportion of Western Europe's population (2018)

# 670

**UK ECONOMIC ACTIVITY PER PERSON (2017)**

GDP per person data based on author's calculations using purchasing power parity statistics.

# £44,468

**US ECONOMIC ACTIVITY PER PERSON (2017)**

Based on author calculations using purchasing power parity statistics.

# 2.4%

Proportion of billionaires from the UK (as of March 2019)

# 54

Number of UK billionaires (2017)

# TRADE: GOODS AND SERVICES

When we think about imports and exports, we tend to think about goods. We can hold a pair of shoes, we can touch a car. But services are intangible. They don't involve any transport. So we tend to discount them a little more when considering trade. That's a shame, because services are important to the UK – they make up about 80% of our economy. And they're important for trade.

What's notable from these figures is that only around a quarter of our imports in 2016 were services, versus 45% of our exports. What's less apparent from these data is that we imported almost £26 billion worth of goods and services more than we exported

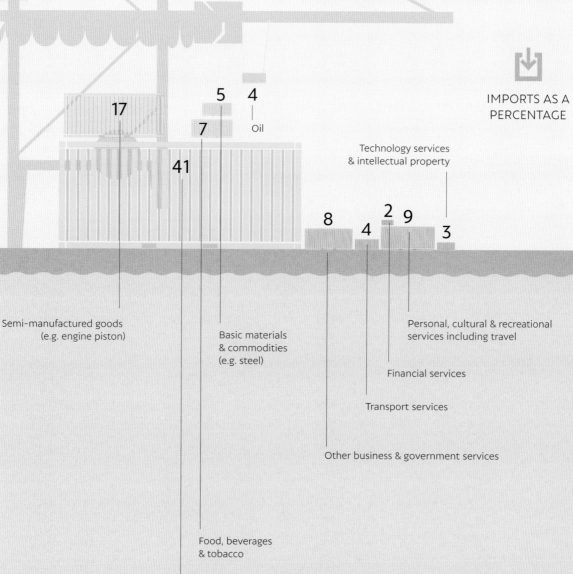

IMPORTS AS A PERCENTAGE

17

5 4

7

Oil

41

Technology services & intellectual property

8

2 9

4

3

Semi-manufactured goods (e.g. engine piston)

Basic materials & commodities (e.g. steel)

Personal, cultural & recreational services including travel

Financial services

Transport services

Other business & government services

Food, beverages & tobacco

Finished manufactured goods (e.g. car)

in that year. That imbalance rests heavily on the goods side: when imports are taken away from exports, £137.4 billion left the UK. The rosier picture is for services, where we made £111.6 billion from trading with the world.

Although some parts of this trade picture are volatile. The price of oil can change rapidly, yet we're still going to keep buying it for the foreseeable future. It's similar for trade in food, where the price is affected by weather and harvests in the UK and elsewhere. Yet point-in-time insights like this provide a reminder that our trade relationships are diverse and span more elements than a cursory look would suggest.

Data from 2016.

EXPORTS AS A PERCENTAGE

Financial services

3

14

4   4

30

6

14

14

Transport services

5

6

Personal, cultural & recreational services including travel

Semi-manufactured goods (e.g. engine piston)

Technology services & intellectual property

Basic materials & commodities (e.g. steel)

Other business & government services

Oil

Food, beverages & tobacco

Goods

Services

Finished manufactured goods (e.g. car)

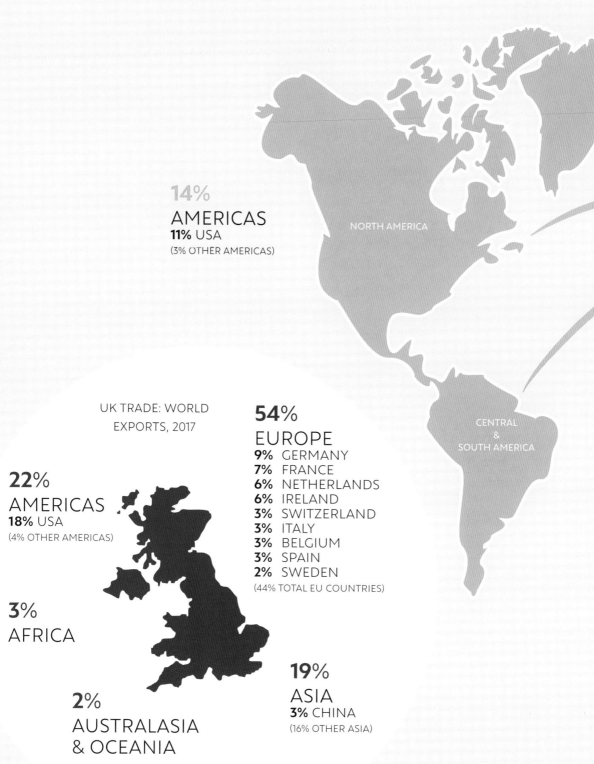

UK TRADE: WORLD IMPORTS, 2017

14%
**AMERICAS**
**11%** USA
(3% OTHER AMERICAS)

NORTH AMERICA

CENTRAL
&
SOUTH AMERICA

UK TRADE: WORLD
EXPORTS, 2017

54%
EUROPE
**9%** GERMANY
**7%** FRANCE
**6%** NETHERLANDS
**6%** IRELAND
**3%** SWITZERLAND
**3%** ITALY
**3%** BELGIUM
**3%** SPAIN
**2%** SWEDEN
(44% TOTAL EU COUNTRIES)

22%
**AMERICAS**
**18%** USA
(4% OTHER AMERICAS)

3%
AFRICA

2%
AUSTRALASIA
& OCEANIA

19%
ASIA
**3%** CHINA
(16% OTHER ASIA)

**63%**
## EUROPE
**12%** GERMANY    **4%** ITALY     **2%** SWITZERLAND
**7%** NETHERLANDS   **4%** BELGIUM   **1%** SWEDEN
**6%** FRANCE       **3%** IRELAND   (53% TOTAL EU COUNTRIES)
**5%** SPAIN

EUROPE

**20%**
ASIA

**2%**
AFRICA

**1%**
AUSTRALASIA
& OCEANIA

## TRADE: IMPORTS AND EXPORTS

'Made in China', or Vietnam, or wherever the new manufacturing hub is based, is a visible sign of imports for a consumer. Yet it provides an incomplete picture of UK trade. For example, in 2017 just 7% of our imports by value came from China. The countries we import from the most in that year were Germany, the USA and the Netherlands, together making up almost a third of our imports. Yet there seem to be far fewer 'Made in Germany' stickers around.

That's because we import a large variety of goods, some of them for business consumption, which the average shopper never sees. And our trade, in general, is concentrated: just 10 countries received 62% of our total import spend in 2017. It's a similar story for our exports where 60% of our export income went to 10 countries. In 2017, the USA topped that list, providing 18% of our export revenue – double that of Germany, our second largest export destination. These two countries are followed by France, the Netherlands and Ireland.

# CONTRIBUTIONS TO THE EU

Now more than ever our relationship with the EU is an interesting topic.

One important element of that relationship is the amount we paid to the EU. There are various elements to this and our contribution included customs and duties we collected on non-EU imports, VAT contributions and a contribution based on our economic growth. To take full account of those contributions, it's important to consider what we received from the EU. That included agricultural subsidies, money for building and infrastructure projects and money to cover the customs and duties we were collecting on behalf of the EU.

And then there's the rebate.

In 1984, the UK negotiated a rebate to our EU contributions due to the make-up of the UK economy. We had higher VAT rates than many EU countries at the time and lower barriers to non-EU trade, both of which increased our EU obligations. Furthermore, our agricultural sector was relatively small so we benefited less from the EU's agriculture funds. The UK and EU struck

## NET CONTRIBUTIONS PER WEEK

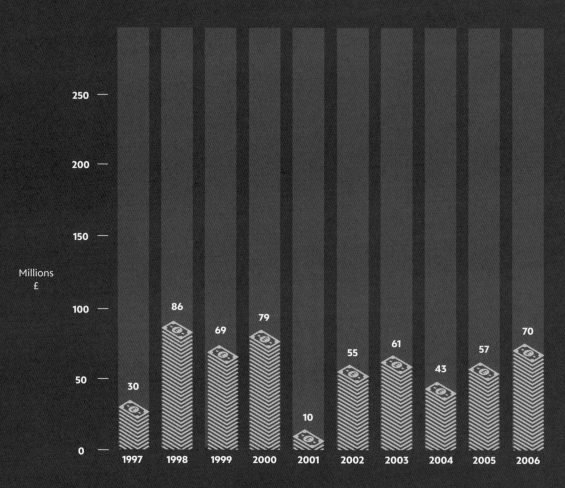

Data not adjusted for inflation.

a deal that included a complex calculation for how much the UK should get back from its original contributions.

When 10 additional countries joined the EU in 2004, they brought with them enlargement costs. In 2005, the UK agreed to shoulder some of these costs via a reduced rebate. This was phased in from 2009.

As such, the EU net contributions (total contributions minus the rebate and receipts) increased notably from 2010 and have averaged 1.3% of total economic activity over the past five years.

The likelihood is that none of this information is likely to change your opinion on Brexit. No matter what figures you put into an EU argument, the truth is that Leave and Remain were (and are) political positions. If you're prepared to pay for Europe, these contributions are worth it. If you don't want to pay for Europe, any contribution is bad. You could be in between, but few of us, I bet, did a cost–benefit calculation.

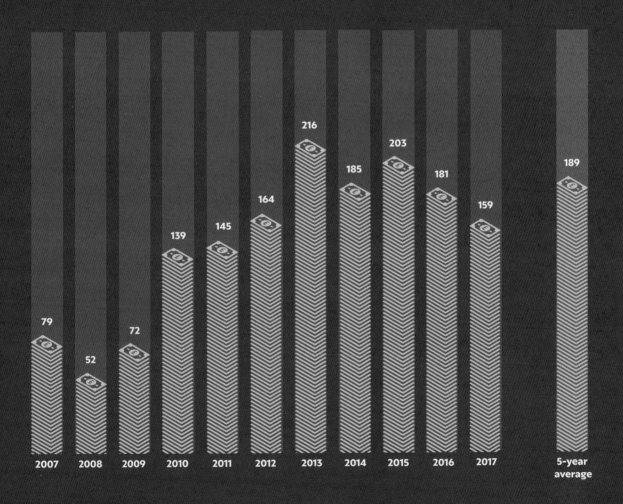

## 2009

ZIMBABWE 7,800

AFGHANISTAN 3,700

IRAN 2,200

PAKISTAN 2,200

CHINA* 1,600

## 2013

PAKISTAN 4,700

IRAN 3,100

SRI LANKA 2,300

SYRIA 2,000

ALBANIA 1,700

## THE MOST COMMON COUNTRY OF CITIZENSHIP BY YEAR

* Data for China excludes Hong Kong.
Rounded to the nearest hundred.

## 2017

IRAQ 3,400

PAKISTAN 3,300

IRAN 3,100

AFGHANISTAN 2,000

BANGLADESH 2,000

# ASYLUM SEEKERS

An asylum seeker is someone who is seeking sanctuary after leaving their country due to actual (or fear of) persecution. This is a politically charged topic that generates plenty of media coverage and strong emotions.

Looking at newspaper headlines, you might expect to see spikes in the number of asylum applications. Yet the data suggest more gradual shifts over time. Citizens from certain countries make up a larger proportion of applications at certain times (it's notable how many Zimbabweans applied in 2009, for example), although it's also clear that there tend to be gradual curves (as opposed to jumps and significant falls) as the situation gets worse and then better in these countries.

Those that come tend to be young – around 3 in 4 are under 35 years old. And in recent years they're more than twice as likely to be men. This might point to the dangers of making such a journey. Or it might reflect the caring responsibilities women tend to have in the societies where asylum seekers come from. Probably a bit of both, plus a whole lot more complexity besides.

If the same applicant reapplies for asylum in the same month, this is counted as one application, but if they reapply in a different month, this would be two separate applications when aggregated to annual figures. This represented approximately 3% of applicants in 2009 and 2013 and 1% in 2017.

## ASYLUM APPLICATIONS BY AGE & GENDER, 2017

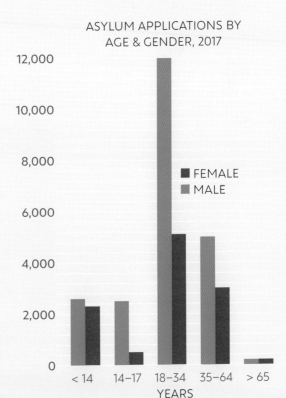

# 9

# LIFESTYLE AND LEISURE

# LEISURE TIME

As a nation we spend almost 40% of our free time on mass media. While the term mass media can include a range of things including reading and listening to music, let's face it, a good amount of that time is spent in front of the box. Although these data do disguise another element: how much leisure time we have.

Men tend to work about seven hours more than women per week. But before male readers get too smug, it's important to point out that these are averages which are skewed by women being more likely to work part-time. Furthermore, they ignore unpaid work, such as caring, cleaning and cooking. And we're not quite at the point of equality in the home.

Women tend to do about eight hours more unpaid work than men. When sleeping and other activities are thrown in, men have an extra four hours of leisure, which they mostly spend on 'mass media'. *Top Gear* anyone?

EATING OUT

MASS MEDIA

# AVERAGE LEISURE TIME (HRS) PER WEEK
## BY ACTIVITY AND GENDER, 2015

● Male  ● Female

PLAYING SPORTS
OR OUTDOOR PURSUITS

CULTURAL
ACTIVITIES

# MEDIA BY NUMBERS

**3 HOURS**

Approximate time spent watching TV per day in 2017*

**2 HOURS**

Approximate time spent watching other audiovisual content in 2017**

**2 MINUTES**

Approximate time spent watching porn per day in 2017

My parents have three or four TVs in a house for two people, yet they only ever watch two. And like most of the country, they're probably watching the BBC, which still dominates our viewing as a nation. As such, it has been difficult for newcomers following a traditional model to enter the market. See the stats here for Channel 5.

Yet we're almost spending as much time watching TV-related content online as we are on a TV (see figures top left). On average about 2% of that time is spent watching porn. Presumably, some people bring up the average by watching way more than others.

Proportion of those aged 55 and over who didn't have a TV in 2018

## 17%

**32%**

The equivalent for 25–34 year olds

## £411m

BBC spending on entertainment programmes (2017)

## £23m

BBC spending on educational programmes (2017)

## 51,73

**TOTAL NUMBER OF TVs IN THE UK, 2018 (TO THE NEAREST 10,000)**

* Excludes playbacks, DVDs, video-on-demand and other videos on TV sets.
** Includes recorded shows, YouTube, video-on-demand, games consoles and other video content.

## 48 mins

Fall from 2013–2018 in the time spent watching TV each day for children aged 4–15

**2 mins:** The equivalent increase for those aged 65 and over

## 1,500

Approximate number of programmes with more than 5m viewers in 2017

## 52%

The proportion of those that were soaps

## 1%

The proportion of those that were sports

## 54

Average age of those who watch BBC soaps

## 28m

Watching the Queen's annual Christmas message is a tradition for many families and interest peaked in 1980, as Charles and Diana Spencer's wedding approached, with 28m viewers tuning in

## 68%

Weekly reach of BBC One (2017)

## 55%

The equivalent for ITV...

## 33%

...and for Channel 5

## 44

Minutes spent on BBC One (2017)

## 30

The equivalent for ITV...

## 8

...and for Channel 5

## 0,000

## 25,836,000

Total number of TV licences in the UK, 2018 (to the nearest thousand)

# TECHNOLOGY AND CLASS

Do you have a DVD player at home? Or did you get rid of one years ago? It turns out that you're more likely to still have one sitting around if you're in a professional occupation.

There's a cachet to having the latest phone or a more sophisticated home entertainment system, but technology changes so quickly and prices tend to fall, so it can be more prudent to wait. As such, it makes sense that those earning higher wages will be more willing to plunge into new technologies while others will wait and make more value-based purchases.

But for many older technologies, the opposite seems to also be true. Those in higher-paid jobs tend to keep hold of their DVD and MP3 players for longer. While those earning less seem to shift from one technology to another. My wife and I are professionals and we have a DVD player and possibly an MP3 player kicking around. It's both discomforting and oddly reassuring to fall into the averages, wouldn't you say?

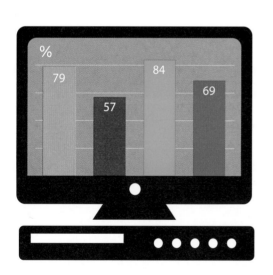

E-READER

DVD PLAYER

| | 2010 | 2018 | | 2010 | 2018 |
|---|---|---|---|---|---|
| MANUAL WORKERS | | | | | PROFESSIONALS |

HOME COMPUTER

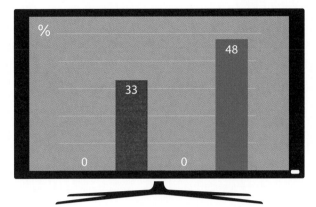

SMART TV

SMART WATCH
WEARABLE TECH

LAPTOP

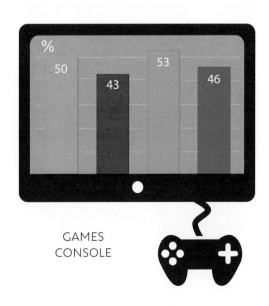

GAMES
CONSOLE

SMARTPHONE

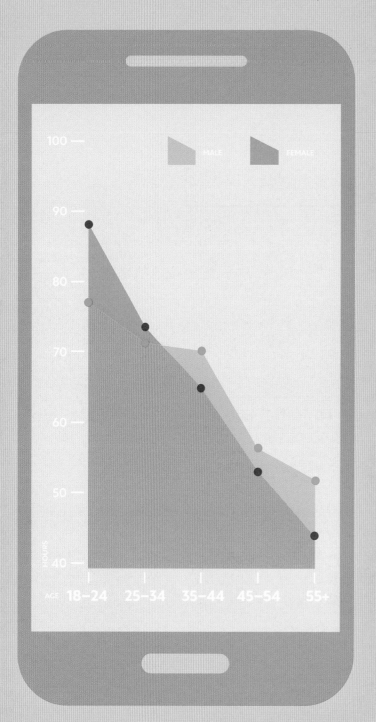

## TIME ON MOBILE DEVICE PER MONTH BY GENDER, 2017

MALE

FEMALE

100

90

80

70

60

50

40

HOURS

AGE  18–24    25–34    35–44    45–54    55+

## INTERNET USE

It's no surprise that we're spending more time online. But the details can be enlightening.

For example, in 2011, tradespeople spent less time online than those in managerial positions – 10 hours a week, yet by 2017 this had evened out. Everyone spends more time online than they used to, but most of the growth in our time online has been among manual workers.

There are other effects. Men tend to spend more time online on laptops and desktops than women do. This is true for almost every age group, although it's particularly stark for those in their late 30s to early 40s. When comparing genders on mobile devices, the notable differences are between age: women spend more time online on their phones than men when they are young, but less time when they are old. This could be due to social networks at different ages or across generations. Yet one thing is clear: we spend much more time online on our phones than we do on desktops or laptops. Most of us have only had smartphones and tablets for around a decade or so, yet they are now ingrained in our lives.

# TIME ON COMPUTER PER MONTH BY GENDER, 2017

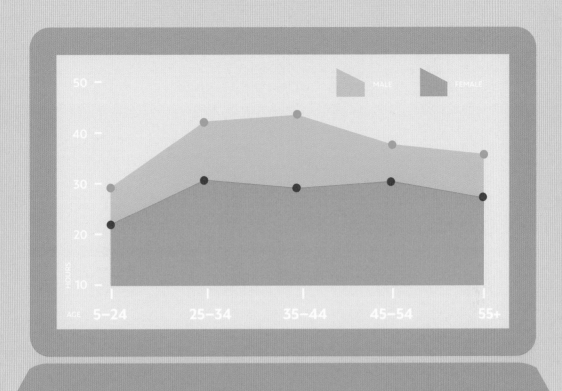

MALE    FEMALE

HOURS

50 —
40 —
30 —
20 —
10 —

AGE    5–24    25–34    35–44    45–54    55+

# GROWTH IN TIME SPENT ONLINE, 2011–17

**19%**
Middle class &
upper middle class

**84%**
Lower middle class

**109%**
Skilled working class

**82%**
Working class
& non-workers

Class levels have been adapted by the author from Ofcom's socio-economic status categories. See Notes for details.

# NEWS CONSUMPTION

Newspapers are in decline and the internet has changed news. You know all about the high-level trends, but what about the detail?

TV is more important than the internet for those over 35 years old and newspapers are relying more on older customers. At the other end, 70% of under-25s received at least some of their news from social media in 2018. Yet other sociodemographic characteristics have a significant effect.

Women are less likely to get their news from newspapers and are slightly more likely to look to magazines and social media. The social media and internet differences were also clear between whites and non-whites in 2018. This could be a reflection of age, as older people in the UK are more likely to be white.

And then there's religion.

There are some significant differences in how people of different religions receive their news in the UK and it's not entirely clear what the drivers behind those differences are. When compared with the general population, a high proportion of Jewish people, for example, receive news from TV, radio, newspapers and (relatively speaking) magazines. And their use of the internet is also higher than the average, suggesting that Jewish people use a range of sources to keep up to date. Sikhs are more likely to rely on radio and magazines than the average and less on TV. Yet where the Sikh community really differs from the average is on the internet: 81% use it as a source of news, utilising both social media and non-social media news content more than the average UK citizen. Christians, by contrast, rely much more on TV as a news source.

Some may fret about these consumption patterns and the trends that underlie them, especially in the light of fake news allegations around the US elections. Yet there seem to be two important factors that are missing from these statistics. The first is how reliable news sources are on each of these platforms and the second is how well each source holds power to account. Reliable news should be able to exist on any platform, but in the past, we've often relied on newspapers and TV to do the investigative work that keeps organisations honest. As these sources become less important for our news, we'll need their internet-based cousins to pick up the baton.

Data from 2018.

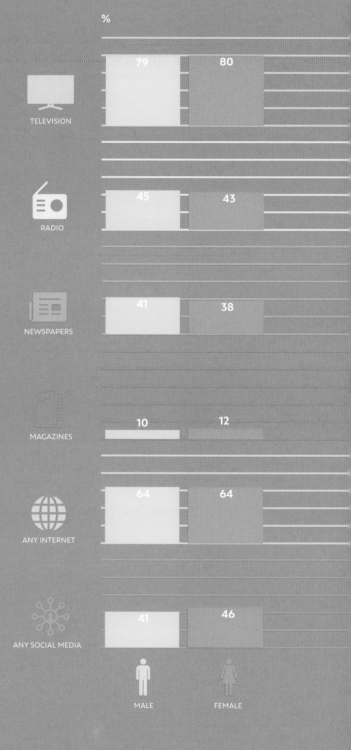

%

TELEVISION — MALE 79, FEMALE 80

RADIO — MALE 45, FEMALE 43

NEWSPAPERS — MALE 41, FEMALE 38

MAGAZINES — MALE 10, FEMALE 12

ANY INTERNET — MALE 64, FEMALE 64

ANY SOCIAL MEDIA — MALE 41, FEMALE 46

MALE   FEMALE

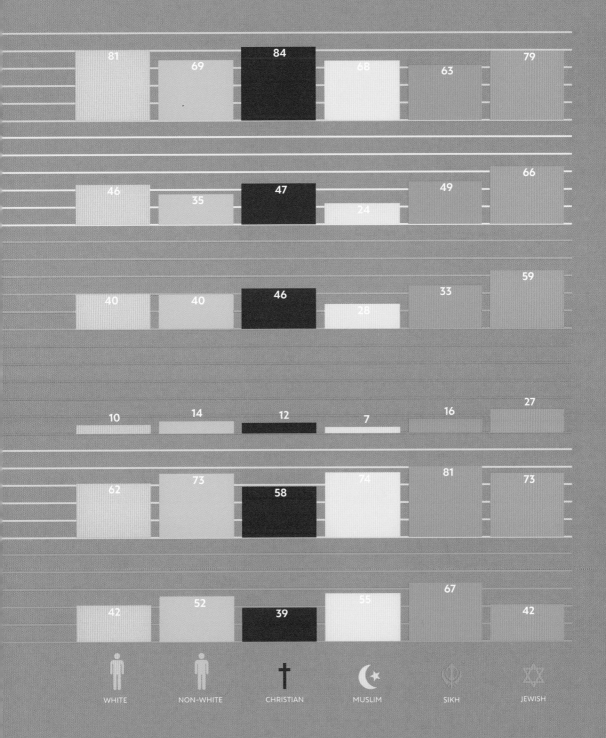

WHITE   NON-WHITE   CHRISTIAN   MUSLIM   SIKH   JEWISH

**18%**
Percentage of households with a cat

**£1.1bn**
The amount spent on cat food in 2017

**1/10**
The proportion of this spent on treats

**1**
The South East's rank for the number of fish ponds

**2**
The number of times more likely a West Midlander is than a Londoner to keep a fish tank

**15%**
Proportion of cats owned by men

**5,000,000**
Number of households with cats

**3,000,000**
Number of fish tanks in the UK

**NUMBER OF PETS IN THE UK 2018 (63.5M IN 2011)**

**51,00**

**1,000,000**
Population of indoor birds and domestic fowl (½ million of each)

**50,000**
The number of people who keep pet mice

**19x**
We spend 19 times as much on food for wild birds as for indoor birds

**1%**
Proportion of households with a hamster

**900,000**
The population of pet rabbits

**0.5%**
The proportion of households who keep lizards (0.1% more than those keeping snakes)

**1st**
Tortoises and turtles – the most popular reptiles

**27%**
The number of dog-owning households with more than one dog

**£449m**
Amount spent on dog treats, 2017

**26%**
Proportion of dogs owned by women

**1**
Staffordshire bull terrier – the most popular dog breed

**200,000**
Population of pet snakes

**7,000,000**
Number of households with dogs

**0,000**

## PETS BY NUMBERS

We're an animal-loving bunch, us Brits, and almost half of all households have a pet. Our favourite pet is most definitely a dog – Staffie is the most popular breed followed by retrievers and Jack Russells.

Dogs make up 18% of all pets, with cats coming second in the list at 16%. And we spend more than three times as much on dog treats as we do on cat treats.

The other two-thirds of British pets are a mix of fish, rabbits, chickens, budgerigars, guinea pigs... In total, we spent more than £2.5 billion on food for all these pets in 2017. And another £200 million on food for wild birds.

Data from 2018 unless stated otherwise.

## SPORT

Almost 2 out of 3 sporting tickets sold in 2017 were to see two teams play the 'beautiful game'. Football is our national sport and attendance at matches outstripped horseracing by more than 6 to 1.

However, attendance at individual sporting events is significant. These benefit from lasting multiple days and having stadia with large capacities. Wimbledon is played over two weeks and 18 courts, for example. And how many spectators can you fit on a golf course?

These data do miss free sporting events, like the London Marathon as, of course, ticket sales are easier to count than people in crowds. But just because a ticket was sold, does not mean an event was attended – these are different things. This is especially true for corporate ticket sales, making these data a little more challenging to collect and adding a margin of error.

*Does not include free-to-attend professional sporting events such as the London Marathon.

**0.8m**
Golf

The 146th Open at Royal Birkdale became the best attended Championship held in England with a crowd of 235,000

**0.9m**
Tennis

**1.5m**
Motorsport

**2m**
Greyhound racing

**2.3m**
Rugby League

2017 saw the biggest crowd ever to attend an ICC Women's World Cup match – over 26,500 people

**2.7m**
Cricket

The IAAF World Athletics Championships was comfortably the best attended UK sporting event in 2017 with over 700,000 spectators

90,000 boxing fans attended Anthony Joshua's world title bout against Wladimir Klitschko

**3.7m**
Other sports

**5.5m**
Rugby Union

**7.5m**
Horseracing and equestrian sports

10m

20m

ATTENDANCE AT PROFESSIONAL SPORTING EVENTS, 2017*

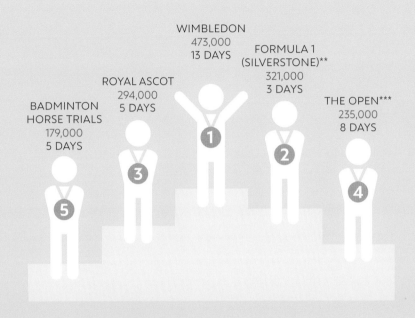

BADMINTON
HORSE TRIALS
179,000
5 DAYS

ROYAL ASCOT
294,000
5 DAYS

WIMBLEDON
473,000
13 DAYS

FORMULA 1
(SILVERSTONE)**
321,000
3 DAYS

THE OPEN***
235,000
8 DAYS

# HIGHEST ATTENDED ANNUAL EVENT FOR EACH SPORT IN 2017*

** 24,000 spectators also attended Fans' Thursday at Silverstone.
*** The Open attendances include 48,000 spectators at the four practice days.

~25m
Premier League

11.3m
Championship

11.3m
Other

30m

40m

47.6m
Football

# THE OLYMPICS

Team GB had stellar Olympic results at both London 2012 and Rio 2016. But how much difference does funding make for Olympic success? Presumably, it's vital to getting top medal slots, although the correlation is not always clear. Funding for cycling increased for both London and Rio, but the medal count didn't follow suit. The opposite happened for swimming between the regular Olympics in London and Rio.

Total medals

Funding £ millions

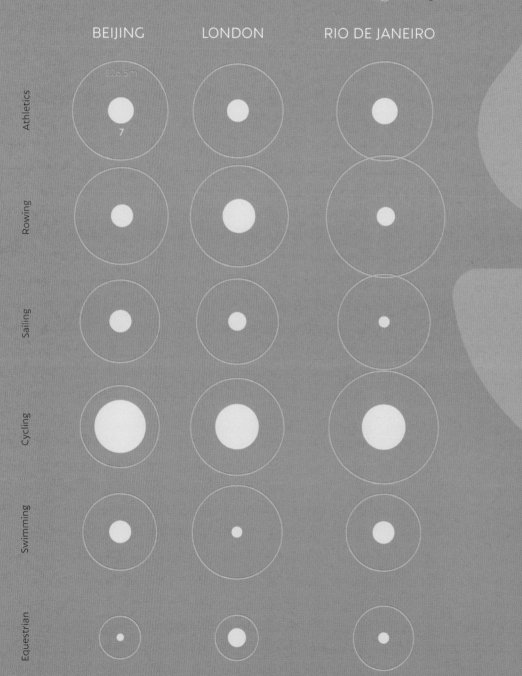

BEIJING    LONDON    RIO DE JANEIRO

Athletics

£26.5m

7

Rowing

Sailing

Cycling

Swimming

Equestrian

One thing is clear, the correlation is strong with the Paralympics.
Although this could be due to a greater focus on the Paras for London
and beyond. It's impossible to consider just Britain in isolation – a
thorough analysis requires data on other countries' funding levels too.
That could be my next book...

Data not adjusted for inflation.

 Total medals

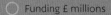 Funding £ millions

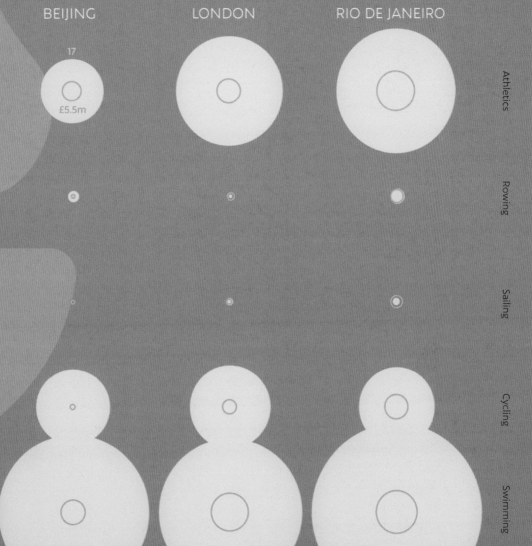

PARALYMPICS

BEIJING        LONDON        RIO DE JANEIRO

17

£5.5m

Athletics

Rowing

Sailing

Cycling

Swimming

Equestrian

10
20
30
40
50
60
70
80
90
100
%

3% 88% 8% 1%  |  11% 70% 16% 4%  |  10% 70% 19% 2%  |  20% 32% 42% 7%  |  17% 65% 16% 1%

## MOST VISITS 2015

■ Business
■ Holiday
□ Visiting friends or relatives
■ Other

## BRITS ABROAD

Remember booze cruises in the early 1990s? People headed to France to buy their allowance of beer, spirits and wine as the price difference made the trip worthwhile. We've since switched continental ferry trips with boot-loads of alcohol for budget airline flights with restrictions on baggage. And we're travelling more: trips abroad jumped by 60% between 1995 and 2005. Holidays still make up the bulk of our travel, but business trips have increased by 50% and we visit friends and family abroad more than we used to. Those family trips are often the longest stays in any location.

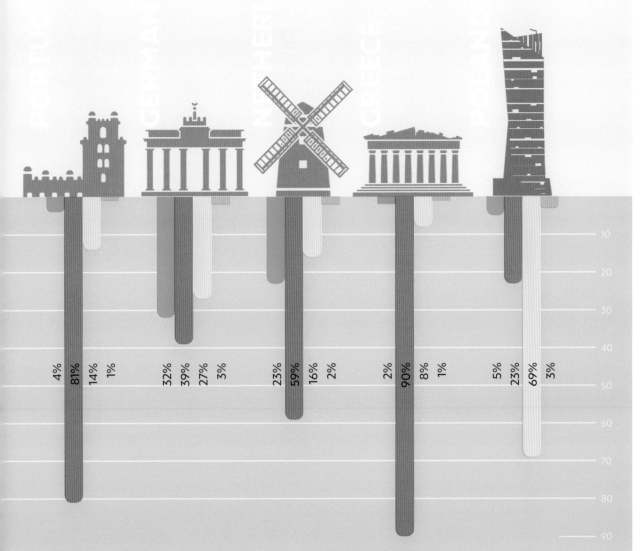

4% 81% 14% 1%

32% 39% 27% 3%

23% 59% 16% 2%

2% 90% 8% 1%

5% 23% 69% 3%

10
20
30
40
50
60
70
80
90
100

%

All this reflects several things: changing prices; different locations; more options via online services instead of high-street travel agents; more Brits living abroad; and more immigrants living in the UK (their family visits are included in the figures). Despite all those changes, Spain and France still top the list of UK holiday destinations. It seems we love to hop across the channel and we still love a beach.

The duration of an average holiday in 2015 remained about the same as it was in 1995. But averages can mask a lot of differences: longer trips are not quite as long as they once were. And these long stays used to be family and friend visits or study trips. These days they are for a larger variety of reasons, including business trips, holidays and a mix of reasons. It could be that we're taking full advantage of visiting family by seeing more of the surrounding area. Or maybe more of us are backpacking and working in places like Australia.

*Continued over page* ➤

## NUMBER OF TRIPS ABROAD

**1995 28m**
**2015 54m**

**1995 11m**
**2015 7m**

As for money, there are different ways to think about how much we spend abroad. The key ones are how much we spend on the trip, how much per day and how much per country. Each tells us different things. It's unsurprising that we spent more in Spain in 2015 than in any other country as it's the country we visited the most. But the US comes second, despite being the fifth most visited country. It seems we splurge more at Disneyland and on Madison Avenue than we do at the Louvre or in the French Alps.

We spent more per day in Luxembourg than any other country, followed by Iceland then Belgium. Over half of all trips to Luxembourg were for business (more than any other location in 2015) and people spend almost two and a half times more per night when travelling for business than the average spend per night. This is not the case for pricey Iceland where 9 out of 10 UK visitors are on holiday. As for Belgium, 1 in 5 UK visitors are on business and more than half are on holiday. I'll leave you to decide why it's number three.

The top five countries where we spend the most per visit are all far, far away: New Zealand, Australia, Thailand, Japan and Barbados. New Zealand and Australia are both countries where we tend to stay for more than a month (on average), which will obviously have an impact on overall spending for the trip. As for the others, it could be a case of why go all that way to scrimp on lunch?

But how accurate is spending data anyway? If asked how much you spent last month, you're bound to round it off to the nearest £100 or so. Even then, you could be way off, neglecting the odd 80p vending machine trip or round of drinks after work. Now imagine someone asking how much you spent on your holiday. And convert those euros into pounds.

The data on these pages are from a sample of people who are surveyed coming through UK entry points, such as airports and ferry terminals. Some questions are easy ('where did you go?'), for others we get a best guess. But as you ask more people, the inaccuracies begin to balance out and the average becomes clearer.

Inaccurate? Of course. The best estimate we have? Definitely.

LONGEST STAYS 1995 & 2015 (AVERAGE BY NIGHTS)

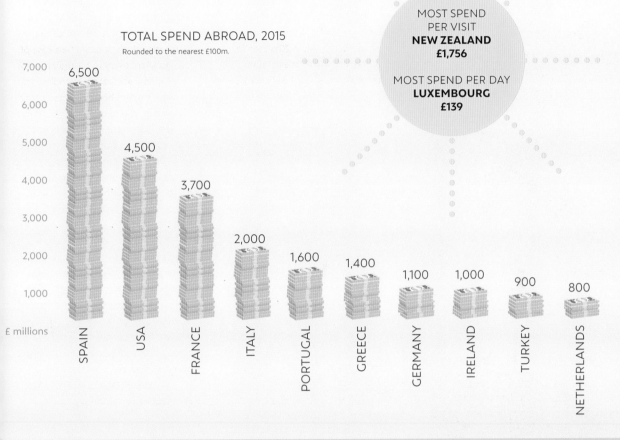

## TOTAL SPEND ABROAD, 2015

Rounded to the nearest £100m.

| | |
|---|---|
| SPAIN | 6,500 |
| USA | 4,500 |
| FRANCE | 3,700 |
| ITALY | 2,000 |
| PORTUGAL | 1,600 |
| GREECE | 1,400 |
| GERMANY | 1,100 |
| IRELAND | 1,000 |
| TURKEY | 900 |
| NETHERLANDS | 800 |

£ millions

MOST SPEND
PER VISIT
**NEW ZEALAND**
**£1,756**

MOST SPEND PER DAY
**LUXEMBOURG**
**£139**

## 1995

TOP 10 VISITS
1. **FRANCE**
2. **SPAIN**
3. **IRELAND**
4. **USA**
5. **GREECE**
6. **GERMANY**
7. **ITALY**
8. **NETHERLANDS**
9. **PORTUGAL**
10. **BELGIUM**

## 2015

TOP 10 VISITS
1. **SPAIN**
2. **FRANCE**
3. **ITALY**
4. **IRELAND**
5. **USA**
6. **PORTUGAL**
7. **GERMANY**
8. **NETHERLANDS**
9. **GREECE**
10. **POLAND**

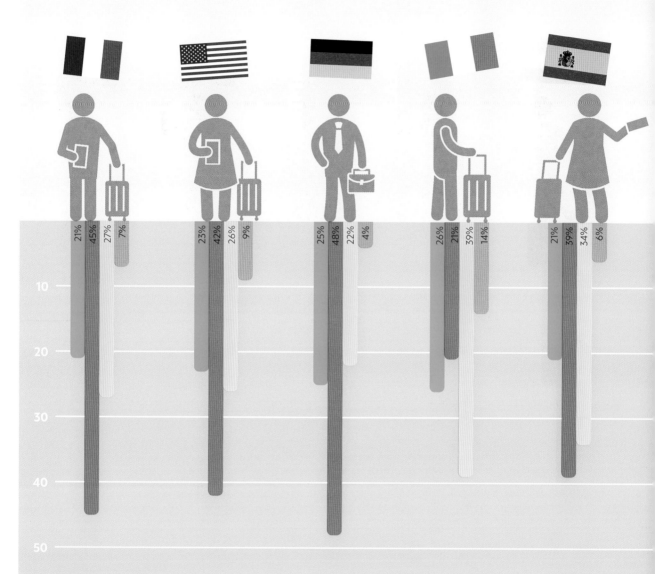

21% 45% 27% 7%

23% 42% 26% 9%

25% 48% 22% 4%

26% 21% 39% 14%

21% 39% 34% 6%

10

20

30

40

50

%

## MOST UK VISITORS, 2015

- BUSINESS
- HOLIDAY
- VISITING FRIENDS OR RELATIVES
- OTHER

All respondents are those staying in the
UK for less than one year.

## VISITORS TO THE UK

People in France love visiting the UK. Or at least that's what the
data suggest. French residents top the number of UK visits in
2015, although visitors from America and Germany were also well
represented. And these three countries alone made up 3 out of
every 10 trips to the UK in 2015. In fact, there were more visits
from these shores than there were from the next five countries
in the visitor rankings.

Such high proportions of visitors from a small number of
countries can be seen across these statistics: in 2015 around 65%
of visits were from 10 countries. In 1995, the top 10 accounted for
more than 70%. Furthermore, the top 10 list has remained pretty

29% 40% 25% 7%

20% 48% 24% 9%

45% 14% 37% 4%

27% 43% 21% 9%

7% 42% 44% 7%

10

20

30

40

50

%

stable over this time. Poland and Australia have replaced Japan and Canada, but the other constituents in 2015's top 10 were all there 20 years earlier.

Yet only around 2 out of every 5 visitors come just to holiday in the UK. More than half are either visiting friends or family or coming for business. And these categories have grown over the years.

From 1995 to 2015, the number of business trips to the UK has increased by more than

3 million to 8.9 million. The number of holidaymakers grew by a similar amount to 13.9 million. Yet the fastest-growing reason for visiting the UK over that period was to visit family and friends. These visits grew by almost 6 million to 10.5 million over this period. Yet the top three countries for family and friend visits are France, Ireland and the USA, which may seem at odds with migration trends over those years.

*Continued over page* ➤

## MODE OF TRANSPORT TO VISIT UK IN 2015

### AIR

72.7%

### SEA

14.5%

### TUNNEL

12.8%

The average stay for visitors in the UK is around eight or nine days, a little less for business, a little more for visiting family and friends. Yet averages can hide a lot of variation. Those coming to the UK to study will obviously stay longer, although the survey used to calculate these data only logs people as visitors if they're staying for less than a year. The other reason why people stay longer is if they're visiting family and friends. In 1995, the average Jamaican resident who came to the UK to visit family stayed for 113 days. Hope you like your relatives...

But let's be honest, the reason countries welcome tourists is because they spend lots of money. The biggest spenders are Americans followed by an unsurprising list of rich countries. Yet part of the reason why visitors from these countries spend so much is because there are so many visits from these countries. There are more surprising results for spend per visit (which measures who goes all-in for a UK extravaganza versus those taking cheaper breaks) and spend per day. The latter is more insightful as it indicates how much people are actually spending when they stay in the UK. And who would have guessed that Estonians spent the most per day in 2015? Or Latvians in 1995?

To be clear, this is self-reported data and imagine how difficult it is to work out how much you spent in the past week or so (let alone converting this between currencies). But it should still be indicative of how much visitors spend in the UK.

JAMAICA
64

SLOVAKIA
46

SRI LANKA
44

PAKISTAN
38

# TOTAL SPEND IN THE UK BY COUNTRY, 2015

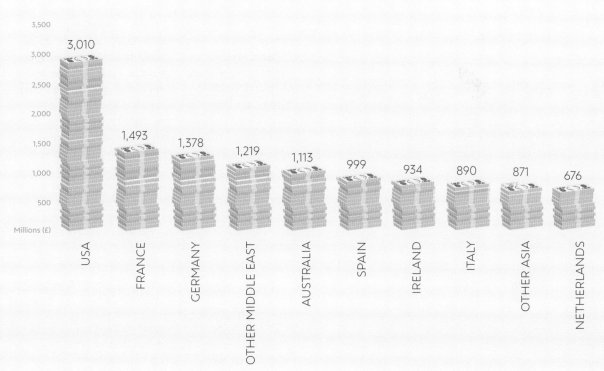

| | |
|---|---|
| USA | 3,010 |
| FRANCE | 1,493 |
| GERMANY | 1,378 |
| OTHER MIDDLE EAST | 1,219 |
| AUSTRALIA | 1,113 |
| SPAIN | 999 |
| IRELAND | 934 |
| ITALY | 890 |
| OTHER ASIA | 871 |
| NETHERLANDS | 676 |

Millions (£)

# LONGEST STAYING VISITORS IN THE UK (AVERAGE BY NIGHTS)

SRI LANKA
36

CROATIA
28

NEW ZEALAND
26

■ 1995

JAMAICA
26

INDIA
22

BARBADOS
21

■ 2015

229

# NOTES

## 1 WHO WE ARE

### Population by Numbers (14–15)

Office for National Statistics licensed under the Open Government Licence v3.0

Ratio of employed to retired people takes the employment level in mid-2017 and the inactivity level for those over 65 for the same period.

Union Flag used to represent Northern Ireland here and in subsequent spreads as it is considered the official flag. No political statement intended.

### Language in Britain (16–17)

England and Wales data: Office for National Statistics licensed under the Open Government Licence v3.0

Scotland data: National Records of Scotland licensed under the Open Government Licence v3.0

Northern Ireland data: Census Office for Northern Ireland (Part of Northern Ireland Statistics and Research Agency (NISRA)) licensed under the Open Government Licence v3.0

Knowledge of a foreign language data: Eurostat

### Immigration (18–19)

Office for National Statistics licensed under the Open Government Licence v3.0

Some residents of communal establishments are excluded from the survey used to create these data, so the estimates differ from the standard ONS mid-year population estimates, which cover all usual residents.

### UK and Non-UK Born (20–21)

Office for National Statistics licensed under the Open Government Licence v3.0

### Immigration by Numbers (22–23)

Office for National Statistics licensed under the Open Government Licence v3.0

Refugee and percentage of migrants data: United Nations

### Major Religions (24–25)

England and Wales data: Office for National Statistics licensed under the Open Government Licence v3.0

Scotland data: National Records of Scotland licensed under the Open Government Licence v3.0

Northern Ireland data: Census Office for Northern Ireland (Part of Northern Ireland Statistics and Research Agency (NISRA)) licensed under the Open Government Licence v3.0

### Losing My Religion (26–27)

England and Wales data: Office for National Statistics licensed under the Open Government Licence v3.0

Scotland data: National Records of Scotland licensed under the Open Government Licence v3.0

Northern Ireland data: Census Office for Northern Ireland (Part of Northern Ireland Statistics and Research Agency (NISRA)) licensed under the Open Government Licence v3.0

### Minor Religions (28–29)

England and Wales data: Office for National Statistics licensed under the Open Government Licence v3.0

Scotland data: National Records of Scotland licensed under the Open Government Licence v3.0

Northern Ireland data: Census Office for Northern Ireland (Part of Northern Ireland Statistics and Research Agency (NISRA)) licensed under the Open Government Licence v3.0

### Population Density (30–31)

Office for National Statistics licensed under the Open Government Licence v3.0

Local authority relates to the following:

England: Metropolitan districts, non-metropolitan districts, unitary authorities and London boroughs

Scotland: Council areas

Wales: Unitary authorities

Northern Ireland: Local government districts

### Oldest and Youngest Local Authorities (32–33)

Office for National Statistics licensed under the Open Government Licence v3.0

Local authority relates to the following:

England: Metropolitan districts, non-metropolitan districts, unitary authorities and London boroughs

Scotland: Council areas

Wales: Unitary authorities

Northern Ireland: Local government districts

### Population Growth by Numbers (34–35)

Office for National Statistics licensed under the Open Government Licence v3.0

### Births, Deaths and Migrations (36–37)

Office for National Statistics licensed under the Open Government Licence v3.0

### Centenarians (38–39)

Office for National Statistics licensed under the Open Government Licence v3.0

Number of people reaching 100 each year is estimated using the number of people who are aged 100 at the mid-year estimates. These data are averaged over two years and divided by two in order to approximate calendar-year occurrences of people turning 100.

## 2 FAMILY AND RELATIONSHIPS

### Marriage (42–43)

England and Wales data: Office for National Statistics licensed under the Open Government Licence v3.0

Scotland data: National Records of Scotland licensed under the Open Government Licence v3.0

Ireland data for 1890: Ireland's Central Statistics Office licensed under the Creative Commons Attribution (v4.0)

Northern Ireland data for all other years: Northern Ireland Statistics and Research Agency licensed under the Open Government Licence

### Relationship Status by Sexuality (44–45)

Office for National Statistics licensed under the Open Government Licence v3.0

### Baby Names (46–49)

England and Wales data: Office for National Statistics licensed under the Open Government Licence v3.0

Scotland data: National Records of Scotland licensed under the Open Government Licence v3.0

Northern Ireland data for all other years: Northern Ireland Statistics and Research Agency licensed under the Open Government Licence v3.0

### Live Births (50–51)

Office for National Statistics licensed under the Open Government Licence v3.0

### Births Outside of Marriage (52–53)
Office for National Statistics licensed under the Open Government Licence v3.0

### Spending on Little Ones (54–55)
Office for National Statistics licensed under the Open Government Licence v3.0

Average annual expenditure per household calculated by dividing average weekly expenditure for all household estimates by seven, then multiplying by 365.25 (0.25 accounts for leap years).

### Family Types (56–57)
Office for National Statistics licensed under the Open Government Licence v3.0

Non-dependent children are those living with their parent(s), and either (a) aged 19 or over, or (b) aged 16 to 18 who are not in full-time education or who have a spouse, partner or child living in the household. Non-dependent children are sometimes called adult children.

The category 'No children' used on the page may include some people who stated they have no children, but actually have non-dependent children.

### Living Arrangements (58–59)
Office for National Statistics licensed under the Open Government Licence v3.0

### Divorce (60–61)
England and Wales data: Office for National Statistics licensed under the Open Government Licence v3.0

Scotland data: Scottish Government licensed under the Open Government Licence v3.0

Northern Ireland data: Northern Ireland Statistics and Research Agency licensed under the Open Government Licence v3.0

England and Wales divorce data by duration for marriages lasting more than 15 years are based on author calculations using cumulative data on the percentages of marriages ending in divorce by year of marriage (1963 to 2016) and by anniversary (table 6 of the ONS release Divorces in England and Wales: 2017).

## 3 HOUSE AND HOME

### Who Builds Britain? (64–65)
Ministry of Housing, Communities & Local Government licensed under the Open Government Licence v3.0

### House Price Growth (66–67)
Office for National Statistics licensed under the Open Government Licence v3.0; also contains HM Land Registry data © Crown copyright and database right 2017; data licensed under the Open Government Licence v3.0

Increase in average house price by start of each decade data calculates an index from 1 January for the first year of each decade to 1 January for the first year of the following decade.

### House Price Changes (68–69)
Office for National Statistics licensed under the Open Government Licence v3.0; also contains HM Land Registry data © Crown copyright and database right 2017; data licensed under the Open Government Licence v3.0

### The Power of Chelsea (70–71)
Office for National Statistics licensed under the Open Government Licence v3.0; also contains HM Land Registry data © Crown copyright and database right 2017; data licensed under the Open Government Licence v3.0.

### The Housing Ladder (72–73)
Residency by ownership data: Family Resources Survey, 2016–17, Department for Work & Pensions licensed under the Open Government Licence v3.0

Dwellings by provision data: Ministry of Housing, Communities & Local Government licensed under the Open Government Licence v3.0

Data to 1990 compiled for the Department of Environment publications: Housing and Construction Statistics, 1980–1990 and 1990–1997

Great Britain totals from 2002 are derived by summing country totals at 31 March.

Data up until 31 March 2014 are for the UK. From this date, these data reflect Great Britain only as the Northern Ireland source table has been discontinued by the Department for Social Development (Northern Ireland)

### Owners and Renters (74–75)
Department for Work and Pensions, Family Resource Survey licensed under the Open Government Licence v3.0

### Mortgage and Renting Costs (76–77)
Department for Work and Pensions, Family Resource Survey licensed under the Open Government Licence v3.0

### Home Ownership (78–79)
Family Resources Survey, 2016–17, Department for Work & Pensions licensed under the Open Government Licence v3.0

## 4 EDUCATION AND EMPLOYMENT

### Education Levels (82–83)
Office for National Statistics licensed under the Open Government Licence v3.0

### Higher Education (84–85)
Office for National Statistics licensed under the Open Government Licence v3.0

### Foreign Students (86–87)
Office for National Statistics licensed under the Open Government Licence v3.0

Combines undergrad and postgrad degrees for both part-time and full-time students.

### Jobs by Numbers (88–89)
Office for National Statistics licensed under the Open Government Licence v3.0

Figures represent last quarter or last month of each year.

### Companies in the UK (90–91)
NOMIS website using Office for National Statistics data licensed under the Open Government Licence v3.0

All industries are based on International Standard Industry Classification codes.

Professional, scientific & technical includes legal and accounting activities, activities of head offices, management consultancies, architectural and engineering activities, scientific research and development, advertising, market research and other professional activities including photographic and translation services.

Business administration & support services includes rental and leasing activities, employment and travel agents, tour operators, security firms, building services firms and other business services, including call centres.

Information & communication includes print and software publishing activities, TV, film and other broadcasting activities, telecommunications, computer programming and consultancy, and data hosting and processing activities.

Other services in the 'Arts, entertainment, recreation & other services' category include membership organisations, repair services, household services where the household is the employer and international bodies.

Health includes health, residential care and social work activities.

### Companies and Industries by Region (92–93)

Office for National Statistics licensed under the Open Government Licence v3.0

### The Great British Commute (94–95)

Office for National Statistics licensed under the Open Government Licence v3.0

Gender split for time taken to travel to work based on author calculations using the proportion of women working vs. proportion of men.

### Employment Trends (96–97)

NOMIS website using Office for National Statistics data licensed under the Open Government Licence v3.0

### Self-employment (98–99)

NOMIS website using Office for National Statistics data licensed under the Open Government Licence v3.0

### Immigration by Occupation (100–01)

Office for National Statistics licensed under the Open Government Licence v3.0

These data use the UN definition of a migrant: someone who changes his or her country of usual residence for a period of at least a year.

Migrants aged 16 and over who did not state their occupation prior to migration or who stated that they were retired, unoccupied or a houseperson are grouped as 'Other adults'.

### Why Immigrants Come to the UK (102–03)

Office for National Statistics licensed under the Open Government Licence v3.0

A migrant is someone who changes his or her country of usual residence for a period of at least a year, so that the country of destination effectively becomes the country of usual residence (UN definition). This definition does not necessarily coincide with those used by other organisations.

Other includes 'going home to live', 'No reason stated' and non-specific answers.

Breakdowns for various countries are available from the ONS website.

### Profession by Gender (104–05)

Office for National Statistics licensed under the Open Government Licence v3.0

### Ethnicities by Profession (106–07)

NOMIS website using Office for National Statistics data licensed under the Open Government Licence v3.0

Sample sizes for 'Gypsy, Traveller or Irish Traveller' are small, so for Northern Ireland, 'Irish Traveller' is output to 'Other ethnic group'. For England, Wales and Scotland, 'Gypsy or Irish Traveller' is output to 'White'.

### Working Hours (108–09)

Office for National Statistics licensed under the Open Government Licence v3.0; data vintage: February 2018, non-seasonally adjusted data

Industry details:

All industries are based on the 2007 Standard industrial classification of economic activities (SIC).

IT & media excludes computer repair (other services), and retail and production of related products (retail and manufacturing, respectively).

Transport & storage includes postal services.

Professional & technical includes legal and accounting services, activities of head offices, management consultancies (including PR), architectural and engineering activities, scientific research and development, advertising and market research, specialist design, veterinary services, photographic activities and environmental consulting.

Administration includes leasing and rental activities (excluding housing rental, which is real estate), employment agencies, travel agencies and tour operators, security and investigation activities, facilities support, cleaning activities, landscaping activities, call centres and business support activities.

Retail & car trades includes wholesale activities as well as wholesale, trade and repair of vehicles.

Health & social work includes residential care and excludes veterinary services (Professional & technical).

These data exclude arts, entertainment and recreation activities and other services. These categories are combined for these data and cover a wide range of activities, making them less easy to interpret.

For people with two jobs, all hours are allocated to the industry sector of the main job.

### Jobs that Pay Well… And those that Don't (110–11)

Office for National Statistics licensed under the Open Government Licence v3.0

### The Gender Pay Gap (112–13)

Office for National Statistics licensed under the Open Government Licence v3.0

### Labour Disputes (114–15)

Working days lost: Office for National Statistics licensed under the Open Government Licence v3.0

Trade union membership: from each union's Annual Report for 2016 from the Certification Office's official list of trade unions

Five largest trade unions infographic not proportional.

## 5 PERSONAL FINANCE

### Household Spending (118–19)

Office for National Statistics licensed under the Open Government Licence v3.0

Total annual household expenditure calculated by dividing total weekly expenditure by seven, then multiplying by 365.25 (0.25 accounts for leap years).

Dry cleaning comes under 'Clothing & Footwear' in the international agreed Classification of Individual Consumption by Purpose (COICOP).

### The Great British Meal (120–21)

Office for National Statistics licensed under the Open Government Licence v3.0

Average annual expenditure per household calculated by dividing average weekly expenditure for all household estimates by seven, then multiplying by 365.25 (0.25 accounts for leap years).

### Looking Great, Britain (122–23)

Office for National Statistics licensed under the Open Government Licence v3.0

Average annual expenditure per household calculated by dividing average weekly expenditure for all household estimates by seven, then multiplying by 365.25 (0.25 accounts for leap years).

### The Great British Night Out (124–25)

Office for National Statistics licensed under the Open Government Licence v3.0

Average annual expenditure per household calculated by dividing average weekly expenditure for all household estimates by seven, then multiplying by 365.25 (0.25 accounts for leap years)

### The Great British Getaway (126–27)

Office for National Statistics licensed under the Open Government Licence v3.0

Average annual expenditure per household calculated by dividing average weekly expenditure for all household estimates by seven, then multiplying by 365.25 (0.25 accounts for leap years).

### Spending on the Home (128–29)

Office for National Statistics licensed under the Open Government Licence v3.0

Average annual expenditure per household calculated by dividing average weekly expenditure for all household estimates by seven, then multiplying by 365.25 (0.25 accounts for leap years).

### Hobbies and Pastimes (130–31)

Office for National Statistics licensed under the Open Government Licence v3.0

Average annual expenditure per household calculated by dividing average weekly expenditure for all household estimates by seven, then multiplying by 365.25 (0.25 accounts for leap years).

### Transport (132–33)

Office for National Statistics licensed under the Open Government Licence v3.0

Average annual expenditure per household calculated by dividing average weekly expenditure for all household estimates by seven, then multiplying by 365.25 (0.25 accounts for leap years).

### Bills and Everyday Costs (134–35)

Office for National Statistics licensed under the Open Government Licence v3.0

Average annual expenditure per household calculated by dividing average weekly expenditure for all household estimates by seven, then multiplying by 365.25 (0.25 accounts for leap years).

## 6 HEALTH AND FITNESS

### What We Eat (138–39)

Public Health England (PHE) and the UK Food Standards Agency (FSA), delivered by NatCen Social Research, working with the Medical Research Council (MRC) Elsie Widdowson Laboratory (formerly known as MRC Human Nutrition Research)

Some food groups are not included due to small numbers of consumers.

Notes about specific food groups:

Meat includes related products and/or dishes.

Pasta also includes rice, pizza and miscellaneous non-breakfast cereals.

Potato includes potato products.

Vegetables relates to cooked vegetables and includes related products and/or dishes.

Buns includes biscuits, buns, pastries, cakes and fruit pies.

Yoghurt includes fromage frais and other dairy desserts not captured elsewhere.

Cereals relates to breakfast cereals.

Fish includes related products and/or dishes.

Salad includes other raw vegetables.

Sauces relates to savoury sauces, pickles, gravies and condiments.

Eggs includes related products and/or dishes.

Sweets includes related confectionary.

Chocolate includes related confectionary.

Butter includes margarine, spreads and some oils which are used as a condiment on bread or salads; however, this food group does not include oils or fats used in cooking.

Sugar relates to table sugar, jams and preserves.

### Disability (140–41)

Office for National Statistics licensed under the Open Government Licence v3.0. Average of financial years 2014/15, 2015/16 and 2016/17

From 2012/13, disabled people have been identified as those who report any physical or mental health condition or illness that lasts or is expected to last 12 months or more, and which limits their ability to carry out day-to-day activities.

### Physical Activity (142–43)

Eurostat

### Exercise (144–45)

Eurostat

Age bands combined using author calculations informed by 2014 mid-year population estimates from the Office for National Statistics.

### Drinking Habits (146–47)

Office for National Statistics licensed under the Open Government Licence v3.0

Where a person drank equally heavily on two or more days, the heaviest day relates to the most recent of these days.

Notes on alcohol units:

No: no units or teetotal

One or two: less than 4 units for men/3 units for women

Yeah, a few: More than 4 units for men/3 units for women, less than 12 units for men/9 units for women

Had a session: More than 12 units for men/9 units for women

Gross annual personal income includes all personal income before deductions for tax, National Insurance etc. It relates to income that is directly received (such as pay, benefits or interest from savings), and does not include income received through a third party (such as a spouse or partner).

The 'Under £10,000' group does not include those with no personal income.

### Smoking Habits (148–49)

Office for National Statistics licensed under the Open Government Licence v3.0

Smoking status is measured by asking all those aged 18 years and above whether they currently smoke, have smoked in the past, or have never smoked.

Average daily cigarette consumption is based on the mean.

### Killer Diseases (150–51)

Eurostat

Notes on diseases:

Kidney-related diseases includes diseases of the ureter and excludes cancers.

Tumours relates to non-malignant neoplasms (benign and uncertain).

Stomach ulcers includes duodenum and jejunum.

Skin-related diseases exclude skin cancer.

Blood-related diseases exclude leukaemia.

Rheumatoid arthritis includes arthrosis.

Hepatitis relates to viral hepatitis and sequelae of viral hepatitis.

Notes on cancers:

Lung cancer includes trachea and bronchus cancers.

Colon-related cancers includes rectosigmoid junction, rectum, anus and anal canal cancers.

Gullet-related cancers are known as oesophagus cancers and are separate from the stomach.

Hodgkin disease includes lymphomas.

Liver cancer includes intrahepatic bile ducts cancer.

Brain cancer includes cancer of the central nervous system.

Kidney cancer excludes renal pelvis cancer.

Oral cancers include lip and pharynx cancers.

Uterus-related cancers exclude other cancers listed that relate to the uterus.

### Suicide (152–53)

Office for National Statistics licensed under the Open Government Licence v3.0

Decade data and suicide by method data are based on author's calculations.

The UK definition of suicide counts 'deaths given an underlying cause of intentional self-harm or injury/poisoning of undetermined intent'.

Deaths in the UK of non-residents are included in UK figures.

Figures are for deaths registered, rather than deaths occurring in each calendar year. Due to the length of time it takes to complete a coroner's inquest, it can take months or even years for a suicide to be registered.

Cause of death defined using the International Classification of Diseases, Tenth Revision (ICD-10) codes. These codes differ slight between England and Wales and the rest of the UK. See the Office for National Statistics' Suicides in the UK bulletin for full details.

## 7 CRIME

### Reported Crime (156–57)

Eurostat with totals for the UK made up of England and Wales, Scotland and Northern Ireland data

Illegal drug trading includes the illegal possession, cultivation, production, supplying, transportation, importing, exporting, financing etc. of drug operations which are not solely in connection with personal use.

### Crime by Numbers (158–59)

Personnel data for judges, police and prison staff: Eurostat

Urinating offences in Scotland: Scottish Government licensed under the Open Government Licence v3.0

Running off without paying offences in Northern Ireland: The Police Service of Northern Ireland licensed under the Open Government Licence v3.0

Blackmail data for Wales and obscene publications for England data: Home Office licensed under the Open Government Licence v3.0

Homicides data aggregated from the crime data for each country listed above (the Home Offices publishes data for both England and Wales)

### Counterfeit Currency (160–61)

Bank of England bank notes: with permission from the Bank of England

Scottish bank notes: with permission from the Committee of Scottish Bankers (www.scotbanks.org.uk)

Northern Ireland bank notes: with permission from the Association of Commercial Banknote Issuers (www.acbi.org.uk)

### High Britain (162–63)

England and Wales data: United Kingdom drug situation: Focal Point annual report 2017, published by Public Health England, Home Office, Welsh Government, The Scottish Government, Public Health Wales, and Department of Health (Northern Ireland)

Scotland data: Scottish Crime and Justice Survey 2014/15, published by Scottish Government

Northern Ireland data: All Ireland drug prevalence survey 2014/15 – keyfacts and bulletin 1, commissioned jointly by the Department of Health (Northern Ireland) (previously the Department of Health Social Services and Public Safety) and the National Advisory Committee on Drugs and Alcohol in the south of Ireland

Population estimates from the Office for National Statistics

Author calculations were required to overcome differences in report standards, categorisations, definitions and time periods.

### Modern Slavery (164–65)

National Crime Agency licensed under the Open Government Licence v3.0

### Rape and Sexual Assault (166–67)

Eurostat, aggregating separate reporting for England and Wales, Scotland and Northern Ireland

### Murder Victims (168–69)

Eurostat with totals for the UK made up of England and Wales, Scotland and Northern Ireland data

## 8 SOCIETY AND ECONOMICS

### Charity (172–73)

England and Wales data: The Charity Commission licensed under the Open Government Licence v3.0

Scotland data: Scottish Charity Regulator licensed under the Open Government Licence v3.0

Northern Ireland data: The Charity Commission for Northern Ireland licensed under the Open Government Licence v3.0

England and Wales data based on the total of the charity by income bands table provided by The Charity Commission as of 30 September 2018 (these data exclude exempt charities, which are regulated by other bodies)

Scottish data based on 'Active' charities as of 19 February 2019

Northern Ireland data based on 'Up-to-date' charities as of 19 February 2019

### Disposable Household Income (174–75)

Office for National Statistics licensed under the Open Government Licence v3.0

Inflation data in text comes from the Bank of England's inflation calculator.

When data were pulled, 2016 represented provisional data. As such, data on this page might differ from published estimates.

### Household Debt (176–77)

Gross disposable household income and population data: Office for National Statistics licensed under the Open Government Licence v3.0

Net lending outstanding and debt data: Bank of England licensed under the Open Government Licence v3.0

Loan amounts outstanding: taken from the Bank of England figures for June, to better match mid-year population estimates

Disposable income levels are gross, consistent with Office for National Statistics calculations of debt to income ratios.

Disposable income levels are not seasonally adjusted, but the figures are an average of four quarters to Q2 of each year. Selecting these periods makes the data more consistent with mid-year population estimates and including four quarters should account for seasonality in the figures.

### The Inflation Basket (178–79)

Office for National Statistics licensed under the Open Government Licence v3.0

Data represent additions to and deletions from the basket of goods measuring inflation on or around the years stated.

### A Cup of Tea and A Bacon Sandwich (180–81)

Office for National Statistics licensed under the Open Government Licence v3.0

Data are derived from the Retail Prices Index from July 1947 to 2004 and from the Cost of Living Index for 1914 to 1947.

From 1948–1967 the prices are for October of each year.

Average prices for August 1914 to February 1915 are representative of 'large' towns only.

The Cost of Living Index began in July 1914, so the prices for 1914 are an average of July to December.

Prices for periods before decimalisation have been converted to pounds and pence.

### Public Sector Workers (182–83)

Office for National Statistics licensed under the Open Government Licence v3.0

Annual figures relate to Q2 data; data includes some projections; changes in headcount are affected company reclassifications from private to public sector or vice versa – a full list of reclassifications is available from the ONS website.

For workers by industry data, HM Forces series excludes locally engaged staff; at time of data collection, England and Wales police numbers were based on projections and subject to revision; HNS data are also subject to revision.

### Public Sending (184–85)

Office for National Statistics licensed under the Open Government Licence v3.0

Secondary education includes some primary school education that is provided by academies that also provide secondary education.

Public debt interest payments reflect gross debt payments minus Bank of England debt transactions. Bank of England debt transactions include its Asset Purchase Facility and Special Liquidity Scheme.

Railways includes the local government subsidy for Transport for London.

Social protection: 40% Pensions; 16% Incapacity, disability and injury benefits; 12% Social exclusion benefits (including Child and Working Tax Credits and Universal Credit); 10% Housing; 6% Family benefits, income support and tax credits; 1% Unemployment benefits; 13% Other

Generic public services: 63% Debt interest payments; 12% Foreign economic aid; 24% Other

Public order and safety: 54% Police; 33% Law courts and prisons; 13% Other

Economic affairs: 32% Railways; 20% Roads; 10% Other transport; 11% Agriculture, forestry, fishing and hunting; 26% Other

Environmental protection: 72% Waste management; 28% Other

Recreation, culture and religion: 35% Broadcasting and publishing services; 27% Recreational and sporting services; 38% Other

Housing and community amenities: 50% housing development; 50% Other

### Public Spending Growth (186–87)

Office for National Statistics licensed under the Open Government Licence v3.0

Data for 2017 prices

### Regional Government Spending (188–89)

Office for National Statistics licensed under the Open Government Licence v3.0

Data represent per person spending and tax figures averaged from fiscal year 2012/13 to fiscal year 2016/17.

Per person calculations are made using mid-year population estimates for the period in which the fiscal year began, e.g. mid-2016 estimates for fiscal year 2016/17.

Expenditure data include current and capital expenditure (minus depreciation).

Taxes from oil and gas are based on revenue by geographic area.

Taxes may include other receipts that are received by the government.

### Tax (190–91)

Office for National Statistics licensed under the Open Government Licence v3.0

Miscellaneous includes taxes on gaming, air passenger duty, insurance premium tax, landfill tax, regulator fees, climate change levy, consumer credit act fees and apprenticeship levy, tax credits (recorded as negative taxes), business rates paid by not-for-profit organisations, and passport fees, among others.

Duties include those on alcohol, tobacco, fuel, business and household vehicles and stamp duty (for land, property and shares).

Corporation tax includes diverted profit tax and is gross of tax credits.

Transfers with public sector are mostly grants from central government, but also include net dividends and interest from public sector, which are often negative for local government.

Other receipts include community infrastructure levy receipts, business taxes payable by local government units (which are recorded as negative receipts) and interest and dividends from private sector and rest of the world.

### Government Debt and Borrowing (192–93)

Office for National Statistics licensed under the Open Government Licence v3.0

### Britain in the World (194–95)

Economic activity, population and PPP data: World Bank

Migrant and refugee data: United Nations

Billionaires data: Forbes

### Trade: Goods and Services (196–97)

Office for National Statistics licensed under the Open Government Licence v3.0

### Trade: Imports and Exports (198–99)

Office for National Statistics licensed under the Open Government Licence v3.0

### Contributions to the EU (200–01)

Office for National Statistics licensed under the Open Government Licence v3.0

### Asylum Seekers (202–03)

Eurostat, asylum applicant counts

## 9 LIFESTYLE AND LEISURE

### Leisure Time (206–07)

Office for National Statistics licensed under the Open Government Licence v3.0

Data provide average time on activity. Time spent on various activities by gender noted in the text are calculated using mid-2015 population statistics for men and women to find total time, then dividing by relevant population figures.

### Media by Numbers (208–09)

All data from: Ofcom, *Communications Market Report*, 2 August 2018, except:

TV population data: Broadcasters' Audience Research Board (BARB) article: Number of TV sets per household

TV licences in the UK data: TV Licensing website, Facts and Figures section

Queens Christmas message data: https://www.telegraph.co.uk/royal-family/0/queens-christmas-message-30-things-didnt-know-majestys-annual/

### Technology and Class (210–11)

Ofcom, *Communications Market Report*, 2 August 2018

### Internet Use (212–13)

Ofcom, *Communications Market Report*, 2 August 2018

'Middle class & upper middle class' includes higher and intermediate managerial, administrative or professional individuals.

'Lower middle class' includes supervisory or clerical and junior managerial, administrative or professional individuals.

'Skilled working class' includes skilled manual workers.

'Working class and non-workers' includes semi-skilled and unskilled manual workers as well as casual or lowest grade workers, and those who depend on the welfare state for their income, including pensioners.

### News Consumption (214–15)

Ofcom, *News Consumption in the UK: 2018*, July 2018

### Pets by Numbers (216–17)

Pet Food Manufacturers Association (PFMA) Annual Reports, 2018

### Sport (218–19)

Paid attendances at professional sports events in the UK data with permission from Deloitte's Sports Business Group, 15 December 2017

### The Olympics (220–21)

Funding source: with permission from UK Sport

Medals data from various published sources including news reports cross referenced with UK sporting websites and Wikipedia.

### Brits Abroad (222–25)

Office for National Statistics licensed under the Open Government Licence v3.0; data vintage: January 2018

### Visitors to the UK (226–29)

Office for National Statistics licensed under the Open Government Licence v3.0

Data are calculated from the ONS Travelpac series, so aggregates may differ from published data.

# ACKNOWLEDGEMENTS

This book was made possible by the excellent graphic design work that Nick Clark and his team at Fogdog completed. Nick, Paul Oakley and Jane McKenna provided help and support throughout the project, were always patient with our comments and redesigns and gracious in fulfilling my design ideas even when, as often happened, I should have left the creative work to those with the necessary skills.

Messrs Nightingale and Pulford (the two Jameses) at Atlantic were instrumental in providing direction, insightful critique and encouragement. They have elevated the final product to nth degrees in terms of design, numbers and text. Emma Heyworth-Dunn at Atlantic provided support and drive in just the right measure at just the right moments. Kate Straker's expertise has guided me through the world of public relations with aplomb. And, of course, Margaret Stead was the catalyst for this whole project, for which I am extremely grateful.

Numerous organisations answered a myriad of data-related questions and gave permission for reproduction of their data. Gillian's flat was a sanctuary for study time. Our conversations on the trials of finishing a book were always a welcome break and often much needed. Phillip's data insights and explanations were ever expedient as well as skilfully and clearly explained. I've yet to find an example where he answered a data question incorrectly.

And thank you to Kate, my wife, agent and number one (1) supporter. Without her, this book would not exist (quite literally). She has made the process easier, relieved the stress and aided the development of this project in every way I could have wanted and ways I never would have thought to ask.

To all of you, thank you. And fair warning: the census is in 2021...

# ABOUT THE AUTHOR

STUART NEWMAN is an Economic Advisor at the Office for National Statistics. He has worked with economic data at the Office for National Statistics for the past four years and has an insider's view on data collection, how the data are compiled and what they are actually telling us. Stuart has an MSc in Applied Economics from the University of Strathclyde.

Published in hardback in Great Britain in 2019 by Atlantic Books, an imprint of Atlantic Books Ltd.

10 9 8 7 6 5 4 3 2 1

A CIP catalogue record for this book is available from the British Library.

Hardback ISBN: 978 1 78649 645 4

Design www.fogdog.co.uk

Printed in Great Britain by Bell & Bain Ltd, Glasgow

Atlantic Books
An imprint of Atlantic Books Ltd
Ormond House
26–27 Boswell Street
London
WC1N 3JZ

www.atlantic-books.co.uk